ROC

BY

TYLER GRINDSTAFF

GRINDSTAFF PUBLISHING

PACIFIC NORTHWEST — 2019

Copyright © 2019 Tyler R. Grindstaff

All rights reserved.

ISBN-13: 978-1-7337817-0-1
ISBN-10: 1-7337817-0-6

This work is copyrighted material. No part of this book may be reproduced, stored in a retrieval system now known or hereafter invented, or transmitted in any form or by any means, electronic, mechanical, including photocopying, recording, or otherwise, without written permission from the publisher and/or author.

Some names have been changed and appearance descriptions have been altered to protect the identities of real people along this narrative.

First Edition

Ebook and Print Edition Available

To my wife,
for without this story, there would be no *us*

CONTENTS

AUTHOR'S NOTE — viii

PROLOGUE — 1

PART ONE
EUROPE

01. TO EUROPE — 10
02. ICELAND — 19
03. FINLAND — 33
04. SWEDEN PT. 1 — 47
05. NORWAY — 53
06. SWEDEN PT. 2 — 64
07. DENMARK — 70

PART TWO
ALONE

08. GERMANY — 88
09. POLAND — 106
10. CZECHIA — 126
11. THREE COUNTRIES — 144
12. AUSTRIA — 150
13. ITALY — 157

PART THREE

HOMEWARD

14. SPAIN	179
15. FRANCE	200
16. BeNeLux	223
17. UNITED KINGDOM	246
18. DENMARK PT. 2	254
19. NORTH ATLANTIC	262
20. HOME	289
EPILOGUE	296
ACKNOWLEDGMENTS	304
ABOUT THE AUTHOR	305

Author's Note

The book you see before you was never meant to exist. In fact, it is a culmination, a kind of snowball, of seemingly independent events which turned a pile of notes and photographs from a trip I had taken what was then a year ago and became a pushing of "there's more."

When I came back from Europe in the winter of 2015 I had a blog which I was posting everything onto. The blog would get read by mostly friends and family, sometimes the world map of readers would illuminate a country like Italy or Iceland depending upon the topic of discussion but it wasn't something I had high hopes for, just a simple way to share some memories. After a couple of months of typing out these simple "look what I saw" blogs I started to have ideas of topics, themes which went beyond my typical text then photo format but delved deeper.

The post which got me fired up was "Solo Women Travelers," a longer opinion piece about the misconceptions I had before the trip and how they were shattered the minute I stepped foot on European soil. I did some minor editing, clicked PUBLISH, then went about my day. Coming back to the blog two hours later, I was astonished to see quite a few people had subscribed to my blog and even more had commented. Women from different parts of the world, maybe five of them, had read the piece and took their time to write out their opinions of what I had written. I was floored.

As soon as I thanked them all and wrote back to their comments, I set out to write more complex stories regarding the amazing trip I had undertaken and the transformative effect it had had on me. By the end of that week I had a dozen blog titles I wanted to write, I felt like I was on to something. I began to take notes, relive the moments which moved me, and wrote at a frantic pace. Soon I had around ten blog posts, each a couple thousand words in length, but felt like I was missing something with the photographs I had taken.

Granted, each blog contained a few photos to help anchor the story, but they were unedited and there were still literally thousands more on my external hard drive. They weren't frivolous photos, but good, well thought out photos taken on a nice camera, which I had bought specifically for the trip, in anticipation of a life altering expedition.

I downloaded photo editing software, watched some free videos online and was soon bringing the photographs, around 10,000 in total, down to a manageable number and making them pop with the reality and awe I kept seeing in my head. I worked on the editing process for the better part of three months, learning as I went and gaining experience as time pressed on. I then installed a publication design software and began assembling the 300 or so photographs into a coffee table book, anticipating a kind of companion to the eventual novel I had been thinking about turning the blog posts into.

The thought of the novel came to me after I had made a list of blog posts representing each of the nineteen countries I had visited during the Europe trip. It seemed silly to use the blog as a kind of disjointed book when I could compile the stories into a coherent narrative and hopefully guide the reader through the experiences which, I thought, helped me grow as a person.

And now, after two years, countless rewrites, editing, learning graphic design, a marriage, the birth of one baby and a second on the way the book is now in front of you. It has been a dream of mine since I was a small child to be an author. That time has finally come.

This book was never meant to be written, the trip was never meant to happen, and life is something we can only attempt to steer. I sincerely thank you for picking up this book, I hope you enjoy.

February, 2019   Tyler Grindstaff

ROOM TO ROAM

Prologue

For the better part of a year my hair had grown long and my life had morphed into one of instability and searching. What I was searching for I couldn't say but the turmoil of the previous months had begun to stabilize and I found myself about to lose my apartment and any sense of normalcy I had previously held.

In the winter previous, my fiancé and I had decided it best to split up and live apart. The idea stemmed from our paths in life splitting from our own psyches. With her reasons explained in all manner of decibels my reasons remained hidden from her but I knew them to be an overpowering sense of not having done enough in my life.

— — —

At 26 years old I had done much of what I had wanted to do. I had gone to Alaska to fish commercially for salmon, had been published in a scientific journal, was about to get my bachelor's degree with two majors and felt good about all that, but something inside me told me to travel, to wander like so many of those other young men in history had done.

In the months leading up to our split an overpowering urge to be footloose came over me and I had begun to think about what backpacking a country or two would feel like, to see new people, places, and things, to smell new air and explore foreign trails. When our relationship cracked I began to think more seriously about a change of pace and after a couple of failed attempts to get back together we both agreed we would both be better off as the always underwhelming "just friends."

It was now late spring of 2015 and my months of confusion and depression had begun to heal and that urge to travel crept up again. The idea had been rattling around my head for a few weeks but I had rejected it based on the improbability of it coming to fruition. It wasn't until a late night, beer-fueled talk with my Turkish co-worker on the deck of the pub underneath the twinkling Christmas lights with the surrounding hop fields the only one's to hear and the night sky full of stars and the big moon looming large above us and our talk turned to Europe and how traveling around like some kind of bohemian hippie seemed to become plausible.

One day I was driving the windy roads to work with the hot sun baking my skin and the radio blasting and the wind rustling my hair like some kind of clichéd American road movie that I said out loud "I'm going to backpack Europe" and I believed myself and I knew it would happen.

I started to tell people of my grand plan to backpack Europe and each person I told in turn told me how they had backpacked here or there or their friend did this or that and what they told them. It was an amazing conversation to be a part of. Everyone was excited and was either reliving one of the best times of their lives or thinking back to a time when they had had a chance to travel but refused for all sorts of reasons.

With each conversation I began to make mental and physical checklists of where to go. Some people told me to pick out a few places and spend a month in each while others told me not to make any plans and let the wind be my guide. With all of these talks my plan of going to a couple countries in Europe for a month or so morphed into a grand adventure, hitting almost all of Europe over the course of three months. I bought a map and began drawing lines to different cities and looking at the geographical layout of a Europe I had never been that fascinated by, discovering which countries were in Scandinavia and seeing which bodies of water lie next to certain countries. It was exciting and freeing but all it ever felt like was a pipe dream.

The more people I told the more the idea became reality but it wasn't until a seemingly typical June day when all of the talk began to gain weight. Up until then the idea of traveling the way I wanted to could only be done solo. I have always been an independent adventurer finding solitude in being alone in all manner of situations. Whether it be hiking miles into a rugged wilderness or taking on a grand project I have always felt a person understands himself better by being put in a precarious situation full of exposure and handling the difficulties of the moment alone.

One late spring day my friend and co-worker Reed Fielding and I were setting up an outside bar to get ready for a concert at the pub we worked and we were talking about where I would go and if I would make it to Scandinavia. I will admit the thought of those Northern countries hadn't crossed my mind as places I wanted to go when all I had been thinking about was Western Europe. After some talk the reason for his inquiry surfaced and it turned out he wanted to go with my on my grand adventure. I was at first, selfishly and foolishly, taken aback at the prospect of having this trip be anything but solo but after minimal pause my entire body felt elated and I agreed and we began talking non-stop of the possibility of us both tackling Scandinavia together.

Soon after our initial conversation Reed had worked out personal hurdles and gave me the official okay to be my partner through the first leg of the trip. Over numerous late night beers the plan for my first two weeks in Europe were beginning to take shape. Together we would hit Iceland, Finland, Sweden, Norway and Denmark then he would head back to the US and I would begin my solo leg in Germany. As for the rest of my trip I refused to make an itinerary of any sort of substance. From everything I had heard over the past months the stories I gravitated towards the most were the ones which centered around spontaneity and not planning anything in advance. These were the Europe trips which seemed the most free and appealed to my own life at that time increasing in restlessness.

It was now late June and with the official decision to travel for about three months in the fall I decided not to renew my lease which meant as of July 1st I would be without a permanent home. On paper the decision seemed at the very least ill-advised but at the time I was relishing in anything that was against the norm. I was a mid-twenties guy who had recently gotten out of a long term relationship, just finished a strenuous bout of college, worked at a tasting room with amazing craft beer amongst a thousand acres of hops and was surrounded by great friends who all worked at the same place. The rules were lax to say the least and I had decided to let my hair grow out in hopes of donating it to a charity of some kind when I returned from my trip. One of my friends had a roommate who was never home so he told me I could stay in his room for the month of July and pay a small chunk of money toward rent. I agreed, my ex-fiancé helped me move out of my apartment, one we had been sharing before the breakup, and I was out at the last minute.

    The caveat of staying in my friend's house was the room wasn't technically mine so my backpacking experience started the moment my old apartment was gone. With majority of my stuff locked up in a small storage unit and a fair amount of this-and-that stuffed into my car I arrived to the doorstep of my new home with the same humungous backpack I would take to Europe. I felt irresponsible being homeless, I felt stupid for not using my degree to get a "real" job, and I felt insecure about not having a plan for the coming months but at the bottom of all the fear was a freedom which was always tingling at the back of my neck and a freshness which I would not have felt if I had done anything else at that particular moment in time.

Less than a week later on July 6th Reed came over and we were searching for the best flights to Iceland. In the end we couldn't leave on the same flight so he would arrive to Reykjavik on the morning of September 11th while I would get there late that night. After all the searching was finished we bought our tickets and had our confirmation numbers and huge smiles crossed our faces. Reed pulled out a bottle of home brew reaching up in the ten percent alcohol range and we toasted to what lie ahead and drank deep from the black liquid while the thoughts of a grand adventure loomed all encompassing, large and free.

The month of July went quickly working long hours with friends during the day then gathering around those same guys at night while drinking some of the finest craft beer we could get ahold of. The freedom of not having anyone relying upon my actions was deafening. If someone wanted to go out after work I would say yes, if someone wanted to get food at midnight or climb on top of a roof and drink beer into the early hours of the morning the answer was always yes. There was nothing tying me down and only experiences and conversations to be gained.

After work my Turkish co-worker and I would talk about his experiences running a hostel in Istanbul and the people he met and what to expect from hostel life and the conversations with people from all over the world and the girls with different attitudes toward life and a strong sense of what it meant to really live.

Soon July was over and the house I was staying in was empty and I found myself truly homeless. The weight of that feeling is something entirely unique but was masked by the friends I had made and the youth which surrounded us. There was always a couch I could sleep on or a party to go to which offered a place to sleep. Reed and his girlfriend were the most generous offering their couch to me on countless occasions. Even my ex-fiancé allowed me to crash on the short couch in her living room and I would wake in the middle of the night with my long legs stretching past the ends of her couch only to roll over and find comfort in my surroundings and felt happy to have such amazing friends and pay a small price for the kind of lifestyle I was pursuing.

The summer flew by with the friends, events constantly occurring at the hop farm, thinking about the trip and relishing in the moment. Soon August came to an end and I submitted my two weeks' notice for work. On the last day, September 6th, the tasting room was full of people, cold beer was pouring and it was beautiful and warm like Oregon is in late summer. My boss let me off early, I bought a beer and walked around the hop farm I had worked for over a year. I walked into the eighteen foot tall hops with their cones plump and green and felt the soil at their base and took a few pictures. The property has a farm house built in 1912 with a gorgeous deck and I walked over to meet my friends and co-workers for a last talk.

We all had excitement in our voices but behind the warmth lay a sadness. All of us knew nothing would be the same once we finished those beers and drove away, me most of all. The entire summer the grand trip felt like something we all talked about but would never actually materialize.

After some last pieces of advice were given we all hugged and I walked off the deck. I went in search of everyone who I had gotten to know so well over the summer and they all gave me their best. My final stop was to the bar and I told Reed "I guess it's not bye to you, I'll see you in Iceland!" We smiled and I walked out. My ex-fiancé had been to the farm earlier and we already said our goodbyes and she gave me a present but told me not to open it until I was on the plane. Once I was in my car I grabbed her package and thought of going against her wishes but resisted.

With a smile on my face I drove past all of the customers and the friends and the life I so cherished and drove on. The next stop was my grandmother's house in Eastern Oregon and the official first day of my adventure began.

PART I

EUROPE

Chapter 1

To Europe

The alarm went off at 4:30 in the morning on September 9th, 2015 the day had finally arrived, I was off to Europe. Climbing out of the king-sized bed at my grandmother's house, I rushed around waking everyone and looking through the luggage I had piled on the kitchen table the night before. Camera, traveler's insurance cards, gigantic backpack, sunglasses, passport, the items were read off in my mind as I ran quickly through the mental checklist I had perfected over the week of packing.

    I had never left the country before so the idea of light travel had never crossed my mind. Days earlier my mom and I had gone to an outdoor retailer and bought all kinds of travel gear for a stay in the rugged terrain of India or some other far flung place I would not be going. The salesman, a stereotype of the want-to-be rugged American adventurer, was quite good at his job and was all but handing things to my anxious mother while I was too excited to intervene. In the end it helped quell our anxieties but did nothing to help lessen the weight of my backpack which had ballooned to ridiculous proportions.

Time clicked by on the numerous clocks hanging from the walls as my mother, sister, and grandmother all groggily helped gather my things into the car, gulp down a steaming coffee, and do a final sweep of the house. We were off to the Pasco, Washington train station in the cold darkness of early fall. The ride was quiet with anticipatory silence everyone lost in their own thoughts of what was to come in the three months I was to be gone. My mind raced with the voyage I was undertaking, the months of talking finally coming to a head, it was officially time to put my shoulder to the wall of expectation and thrust myself headlong into whatever was to come.

We arrived to the train depot early and waited on a hard, uncomfortable wooden bench. These three women meant the world to me and I was pleased they were there amidst all the lonely souls which inhabit a train station at that time of morning. With the approach of my train we all said goodbye for now and my mother started to cry. The sight of her tears helped bolster my idea of what I was undertaking and made me smile with the love she was emitting. Hoisting the giant backpack to my fresh shoulders I walked along the corridor toward the steaming train, not looking back but only looking forward.

From Pasco, the train steamed along the Columbia River in the early morning darkness which gave way to a brilliant sunrise and an astounding view of Mt. Hood in the distance. We had a layover in Portland and I struck up a conversation with an older man about the adventure I had just started and he told me about a similar backpacking expedition he undertook in the seventies. The man and I talked for the better part of an hour about the sights he had seen, the women he had had, and the life he had led since that trip, a life made better by finding a part of himself in Europe and the beauty of living a life without regret. We both boarded the next train bound for Seattle and continued our conversation until it naturally died out and I looked out the window at the beautiful Pacific Northwest landscape, the same landscape I have always lived amongst, passing by and a kind of sadness overtook me as I contemplated the idea of leaving my home.

 Once in Seattle, I found my way to the airport, made it through security, and had a few hours to spare. I spent my time sitting in a wooden rocking chair watching the planes take off and taking notes on my trip thus far for a reason I had yet to figure out. Night had fallen on the runway and I made it to my terminal, we boarded, and we soon took off into the night on my first red eye flight. It was awkward sleeping in a plane seat and I only managed to get maybe an hour of rest before we touched down at JFK airport.

With eyes burning I navigated my way out of my airline's terminal and went in search of the next flight, a flight that was many hours to take-off. I spent the morning walking everywhere I could without leaving the security checkpoints and with a couple of hours before take-off I decided to check-in to my flight. I went to the check-in and the lady asked me how my day was going, I said "amazing, I'm going to Iceland today!" which she replied "Not today you're not."

My stare must have screamed shock since she explained her reasoning behind her sassy comment. Apparently most foreign countries, especially Europe, won't allow travelers into their borders without a return ticket or a ticket out of their country. In my wandering hippie ways I thought it would be totally fine to book a one-way ticket in then book a return flight when the time was right. It turns out I was wrong.

The lady behind the counter informed me of the process; if America lets the traveler go to their destination without a return ticket the traveler will be stopped at customs in the foreign country, sent back to their country of origin, then the airline which sent said traveler gets a hefty fine. With every one of my sweat glands on fire she gave me two options before I could pass; the first was to book a ticket to Finland (our next country after Iceland) then cancel it later OR decide on a return ticket to America, date and all, on the spot. I chose the latter, which in retrospect was a good decision so the I had a finite amount of time in Europe. After buying the tickets in the airline ticket office I was back to the sassy lady's desk with a confirmation firmly in hand.

Security was a breeze and I changed out of my pajama pants and into real clothes. After a few hours dealing with currency exchange and credit card activation issues I was in line at the gate to go to Iceland. The plane was delayed by half an hour but once all systems were go my heart began race and the all-too-familiar sweat glands began to pour. I was past the point of no return.

The plane departed JFK and we flew into the afternoon sky officially starting the fantastic voyage I had been anticipating for months. So many emotions washed over my stress-ridden brain as the ground grew small beneath us and the clouds engulfed us like we were nothing. It was to be a direct flight to Iceland and I had a window seat and despite all the worrying and stress the adventure had taken off right as scheduled.

With water blue beneath me I turned my focus to the screen in the seat rest in front of me and spent the next several hours switching between watching a movie and looking at a real-time map of our progress across the world. It made me think back to months earlier when I had placed a giant map of the world on the wall of my small apartment and began tracing a proposed route across Europe. I had bought the map shortly after Reed and I had bought our tickets to Iceland so I knew where the start of the journey would begin. After I drew that initial line from New York to Iceland my pen hesitated, I had no idea where I would be going next and it was thrilling. From there I would mark shaky lines this way and that only to erase them back to the original line in Iceland. The pen always found its way back to the beginning, anything further would take away from the spontaneity, the heart of all the best stories I had heard for months before. After a week of throwing curious glances at the map and standing on my couch to get as close as possible so I would be literally face-to-face with the world, I decided I would make it up as I went.

Thoughts of those times in the apartment seemed like years ago as the plane sped across the ocean, inching ever closer to Scandinavia. I watched as the ocean turned into Greenland then back into ocean then soon day turned into night. People around me started snoring and the cabin lights dimmed. I thought of sleeping but every time I closed my eyes thoughts of what I was hoping to come in the next three months would flash across my mind and the nervous excitement would jolt me awake.

As I sat rubbing my eyes after a bout of turbulence woke me a young girl, I think American, was looking out my window from across the aisle and asked what those strange lights outside the plane were. She crossed over into the empty seat next to me and we both smiled broad as the green lights stretched ethereal across the black backdrop of the sky. It was Aurora Borealis and she was every bit as beautiful as people say. The young woman and I sat silent for many minutes as the Northern Lights shimmered until we finally gained our composure and she went back to her original seat. I watched those lights for what seemed like an eternity. I had spoken with people who had been to Iceland for many days without seeing the Northern Lights and here I was seeing them before even landing in Scandinavia plus with a crystal clear night the Lights took on such a polished finish as the greens danced across the night sky.

Within an hour we were landing at the Reykjavik airport, it was almost midnight and I had no cell phone reception and absolutely no idea what was to happen next. The girl across the aisle said she was from New York and it was her first time out of the country so we decided to team up in order to gather our bearings and escape the shell shock of our situation. The airport had few people lingering within and after we grabbed our luggage, both of us sporting gigantic backpacks, we found our way outside.

It turned out the girls name was Sarah and she was in her mid-twenties with mousy brown hair and a cute face. She had tired of the monotony of adult life back in New York so she decided to go an adventure, a solo trip to Iceland for a week. In rapid succession she explained she had just gotten over a rough break-up, bought a ticket to Iceland, was going to rent a vehicle, drive the "Golden Circle" around the country sleeping in the back of the ATV, then fly back to New York ready to tackle whatever came next in her life. I stood in awe. Here we were, two people from entirely different backgrounds with similar stories meeting each other randomly at the precipice of our grand adventures.

I left the girl at a car rental hut on the airport's curb with her wide eyes showing fear and excitement and trepidation all in equal measure. Nearby I found a shuttle hut, paid for a ticket in Icelandic currency, and hopped on a bus in the shining parking lot. As I boarded, my phone connected to a phantom wi-fi and a series of texts came in from Reed instructing me what to do once I arrived to the airport. Soon the bus was flooded with teenagers from a local high school chattering in Icelandic and looking at me with intense scrutiny, I was the only one on that bus not from Scandinavia and everyone was acutely aware of it.

The bus drove the hour or so from the airport into Reykjavik with the night sky gleaming from the billions of stars above us. I thought of my journey over the course of the past couple of days. Starting on a train in small town Washington and now I was crossing lava plains in Iceland. It is truly amazing what a person can do with a bit of blind ambition.

Around 2 am my shuttle dropped me off at a hostel with lights on and a sleepy young girl reading a book at the front desk. In a daze from the journey I had just undertaken, exhausted from hours of restlessness, and a general lack of knowing what I was doing I bumbled through a check-in process made much simpler by Reed booking my bed when he arrived the day before. Relieved, I found a set of lockers meant for luggage but soon realized my gigantic hiking backpack was twice the size of a single locker and had no chance of fitting it inside. Wanting nothing but to sleep, I trudged up the stairs of the hostel with heavy backpack in tow, found my room and gently opened the door to a cacophony of snoring and the tremendous stench of wet feet hitting my nose with full force.

Through the darkness I found my empty bunk, a top bed, and quickly proceeded to drop my backpack onto the metal heater with an impossibly loud clang. A snarl of frustrated snores and coughs and a "Wasss 'at" raged from out of the darkness as I blearily climbed to the top bunk hauling my monstrosity of a pack with one last rush of pissed-off exhaustion.

In the darkness of the room I made a kind of nest and looked at my phone. It was 2:30 in the morning and I was in Reykjavik, Iceland. Simultaneously my brain raced with thoughts of where I was and how I had gotten there and the aching drowsiness of the lack of sleep I had forced upon myself on the voyage from west coast America.

Somewhere in that sleeping darkness was my friend Reed and just outside those thin hostel walls were myriad adventures waiting to be had. After months of talking we were standing at the brink of whatever Iceland would bring. I closed my eyes that night in Iceland with a smile on my face and a glow in my soul. Like that girl I had met on the plane I too was living out an adventure with no telling where it would lead.

Chapter 2

Iceland

A gleaming white light shone in through the sheer curtains of the hostel room awaking me from the comatose sleep which was no where near long enough to be restful. It was 7:30 and most of my anonymous roommates had vacated the stinking dormitory leaving a few of us with arms draped over eyes and loud noises coming from numerous unseen crevices. With the rush of excitement from the mystery of what the day would hold, I grabbed my stuff and left the room much more quietly than I had entered only hours before.

The hostel was calm in the morning air as I descended the staircase. A large variety of shoes and boots lined the sides of the stairs giving a glimpse into the personalities and ambitions of the people taking up temporary residence in the eclectically furnished building. I walked into the common room to see my friend and now traveling companion Reed in an overstuffed chair sipping a coffee from the bar behind him. A thick blue flannel shirt draped over his wiry frame while his close cropped, black hair, cut himself days before, offered a striking juxtaposition to his piercing blue eyes. Once I saw him I couldn't help but giggle, trying and failing to restrain the flood of emotions swelling within my body. After months of talking, hours of travel, and many near panic attacks we were looking at one another in a hostel in the first country of our voyage. I pulled a chair zealously toward my friend and we spoke quickly, at least on my part, Reed's pattern of speech rarely leaves his zone of moderate-speed comfort, of the hurdles we had to overcome in order to be where we were.

Reed had arrived the day before, mid-morning, and decided to survey the city. After stopping for coffee at a quaint cafe, he walked all over the downtown area, bought a traditional Icelandic sweater for an amount of money he deemed to be fair but suspected was exorbitant due to the currency conversion, and came back to the hostel for an early night's rest. As we talked I realized how little rest I had gotten throughout my ordeal but I shook it off with a cup of black coffee and a bagel.

Not wanting to waste a minute of our day we exited the hostel and walked out into the crisp morning air and walked along the snow covered sidewalk of a new country. It is hard to describe how it felt to be so far away from home with someone I had become such good friends with. I had met Reed only a year before when he began working at the same craft beer pub I had been for the better part of a year. It was a full-day of training on the Oregon Coast at the main brewery and we spent over twelve hours together talking about beer, our lives, and the experiences we had gathered up until that point. By day's end we had found another drinking establishment and kept the conversation, and the pints, flowing. Our backgrounds were very much different but at the end of the day we found so many similarities in our interests that we were more than excited to get to working together.

Over the course of the next year we saw each other almost everyday. While working together we passed the time discussing our dreams and aspirations, the women in our lives, and places we wanted to travel. Sometime around April these talks of travel, mixed with the international clientele our pub drew in, began to coalesce into semi-solid states. It was then the idea of traveling around Europe started floating around my mind and in a matter of a week I was sure I would make it a reality before the year came to a close. Settling on Iceland as the first country, I informed Reed of my tentative plan one day while setting up an outside bar for an event at the pub. In our nonchalant manner of speaking to one another I invited Reed to join me and within hours, and an okay from his long-term girlfriend, it was settled; he and I would be crossing the globe to explore Scandinavia together.

From then until June it was all I thought about and the entirety of the discussions Reed and I had over so many pints of beer. The conditions couldn't have been more perfect. I had been broken up with my long-term girlfriend since the beginning of the year and was looking for something stupid to do in order to keep my mind off of her. Traveling the world seemed to be just the thing I needed.

While living with a friend from work Reed and I bought our tickets making our trip a reality. The last day of work, three days before I boarded the train starting the journey, I told Reed good-bye from the other side of the bar. Less than a week later he and I were walking the streets of Reykjavik nearing a large church with sloping edges reaching for the sky.

We entered the beautiful church and noticed we could ascend to the top for a small fee. I reached into my wallet and pulled out the five euro note which had been given to me by a European man visiting the pub in the middle of the hop fields over the summer after hearing about my trip saying, "here ya go, this out to buy you a train to somewhere!" The bill was crisp as I handed it to the ancient woman stooping painfully at the ticket booth.

Reed and I ascended the elevator to the top and were greeted with a magnificent view of the city. The clouds had lifted on the seaward side giving way to scattered blue skies and a large rainbow arching colorful over ships and succinct buildings down below. We surveyed the city from up high and pulled out my camera beginning the first of what would become thousands of photos from the trip.

Reed pointed down at buildings and neighborhoods he had visited the day before smiling ever so slightly as he pridefully gave a bit of history on this museum or that piece of knowledge, he had done his homework. Making our way to the other side of the observation area we looked out into the countryside with its dark grey clouds fully formed dropping sheets of rain in some parts of the lush green countryside. We looked at each other knowingly; that was our next destination.

One of the ways Reed and I are the most common is our sense of adventure. Not the simple, leisurely kind of adventure, we enjoy the masochistic kind, the kind where being uncomfortable and slightly hoping for something not-so-bad to happen just might happen. It was this shared trait which made us giddy as we hurried back to our hostel, grabbed our things, and rented a car to go into that storm which lie ahead of us. My heart leapt as we were shown the car, a small European hatchback we dubbed "The Getz."

In a normal situation this car would be considered a piece of shit on wheels but since we were in a different country and it would give us autonomy over our destiny we couldn't have been more proud of the windshield cracks and duct taped mirrors which gave it so much character. Without giving much thought to the paperwork and totally denying the insurance plan we were handed the keys, threw our bags into the back and drove out of the parking lot ecstatic.

Without incident we navigated our way through the minimal traffic of Iceland's largest city and soon found ourselves driving into the rugged, green countryside which seemed to stretch endless on all sides. It seems so simple, but the act of driving in another country is amazingly fun. The traffic in Iceland is the same as in America, we drive on the same side of the road, we obey basically the same laws, but there was something about the freedom of a vehicle and the possibilities inherent within which made every mile travelled a direct example of our own choosing. If we had taken a bus it would have been a there-and-back trip, there wouldn't have been room for spontaneity or creativity but in the Getz it was up to us which route to take, which sight to see, how much time was spent at each destination. With the radio emitting local Icelandic channels we switched between incessant chattering, mostly on my part, and quiet musings out the window at the green vastness and mysteriously placed boulders scattered across open fields.

Iceland was the country Reed had wanted to visit the most and because of this he had made an ambitious itinerary which was to be democratically decided into a practical route around the southwest corner of the country. First on the list was Thingvellir (Þingvellir in Icelandic), the sight where two tectonic plates (the North American and the Eurasian) are coming together which manifests itself in a kind of canyon of rugged rocks covered in thick green moss. We arrived in Thingvellir and were astonished at the length of the crack in the earth and quickly descended into the bottom of it. Lush green moss padded our tracks as we navigated over invisible holes and over sharp, lichen sprinkled rocks feeling like true explorers. To our surprise there were no other tourists anywhere and it felt like we had the entire tectonic plate boundary to ourselves.

After an hour of climbing around and listening to Reed chatter off historical facts of the area we ascended one of the walls and were met with a sign printed in both Icelandic and English telling tourists to NOT descend into the crevice. Feeling bad about our traipsing over trespassed ground we hurried off to another part of the park, a waterfall of deep blue water crashing amidst rocks with its spray misting tourists which must have avoided the crevice from before. On our way back to the car we met a few young women from some part of Europe and told them about our plans for navigating Scandinavia and I felt the gravity of my three month trip for the first time. When I was making marks on my world map in the apartment it didn't seem like such a big deal but now at the start of this expedition actually talking it out to complete strangers and seeing the reactions on their faces it was real, it was happening, and it was only day one.

    The girls went their separate ways and we found our car with a real Icelandic sheep munching on greens not far from it. Reed wanted a picture of him with his over-priced Icelandic sweater on and a real Icelandic sheep next to him and I took the photo with a thorough glee in my heart; true tourists. We climbed into the car and it was my turn to drive.

    The next stop was a town called Geysir which, not surprisingly, was home to a large water-spurting geyser. Tourists were crowded all along the hole in the earth all of us waiting anxiously for the big moment when a burst of water would erupt from the hole. The big moment arrived and everyone said there "ahhhs" and "ohhhs" and then went back to staring at their phone screens hoping to have gotten the perfect shot. Not digging the crowd, we climbed a hill to get a better view of the geyser, still weren't too impressed, then got back into the Getz and headed on down the road.

    After a quick stop at a gas station we found ourselves back in the countryside cruising along listening to Icelandic music. We came to a large parking lot with even larger off-road vans with adventurous sounding business names printed all along their sides in sharp, monstrous, EXTREME font. A short hike brought us to the rainbow-covered waterfall of Gullfoss with its throngs of tourists in bright yellow parkas taking photos of themselves with selfie sticks and a countless number of peace signs thrown up for good measure.

It was mid-afternoon when we left the gigantic waterfall and found a convenience store, ate a couple questionable hot dogs with some chips and drove along the Golden Circle highway to the far southern end of Iceland. The Golden Circle is the main highway which wraps around Iceland in one continuous loop. Like the girl I had met on the plane over, many people drive the entirety of the road since it traverses all the geography Iceland has to offer. On our voyage down the Circle we were both surprised at how many sheep were wandering over the roads, including ones being herded by ranchers atop miniature horses. Passing big-wheeled tractors and bridges with one lane, we trudged along the highway admiring the serene beauty and once we reached the southern end we understood the reason so many people have that vast country on their bucket list.

As we turned to head east I watched as the ocean's surf washed up over black sand beaches offering a stark contrast to the snow-covered hills on the other side of our car as we sped down the highway. We stopped to admire Eyjafjallokull but the mighty volcano was hidden behind a thick cloud cover acting as the Joker card to a day of perfection.

The next couple of hours was spent visiting two more beautiful waterfalls on Reed's itinerary followed by a stop at a few man-made caves with dwellings inside called Rutshellir.

A beautiful sunset burned bright orange behind the rumbling ocean as we sped along the Golden Circle to the town of Selfoss where we had booked a guesthouse. Along the way we searched the skies for the Northern Lights but were denied due to cloud cover which thickened as we neared our destination. My companion still hadn't seen the electric green of the northern beauties and was jonesing for the fix which itches at the eye sockets of every visitor to the great North. While in town we searched for places to eat but were let down to only find a burger spot which was closing soon. We ate quickly, bought some cheap Icelandic beer from a gas station, and set out to find our guesthouse. Rolling down a long gravel road lined with trees we pulled over and searched the skies once again for the Northern Lights through gaps in the grey clouds. No luck.

The guesthouse was quiet with a few lights shining through the big windows of the main house. Sheepishly we walked in the door and were quickly told the entire site was welcome for a dinner but being tired and, at least on my part, new to the communal scene we declined and found our small cabin-like room. Walking in, the large square room housed a queen sized bed plus a bunk bed in the corner. I took the large bed and Reed volunteered for the bottom bunk. Room temperature beers were pulled from my bulging backpack and we sipped the contents with glee.

Both exhausted from the meandering journey of the day, we chatted off and on about the next days sights while drinking from the tall, green cans. It couldn't have been too late when jet lag caught up to us and the lights went dark in our cabin. Sleep came down upon me like a hammer and before I knew it that peculiar Icelandic light was shining in from the curtains once more and adventure was calling.

After a shower, I reloaded my backpack and soon realized how ridiculous its size was. Back at my grandmother's house I had packed it like I was going on some kind of African safari, the kind where a person wouldn't see another person for months. I hadn't realized it, or maybe it was my way of dealing with the anxiety, but traveling Europe didn't require a gigantic hiking backpack full of stuff to get by. Slightly embarrassed at my lack of travel acumen I quickly threw my hulking bag in the back of the Getz and climbed into the front seat. Reed, having travelled much more than I, had packed a school-sized backpack and a small duffle bag for the trip. It must have been obvious to anyone with a decent set of eyes which of us was the better traveled.

The morning was drizzling rain which made the green covering all around us seem that much more lush and fitting for our Scandinavian journey. In preparation for the trip Reed had taken to reading the works of Snorri Sturluson, an Icelandic poet and politician who lived in the 12-13th centuries. Snorri kept a home and died in Reykholt, a city which now houses his official museum. It was a place my companion had been wanting to go and, since traveling is very much like a marriage, I consented to visit the museum in hopes of learning more about this famous figure of Icelandic history not to mention gain favor for a preference of mine in the near future. The museum was educational and after an hour or so of looking at paintings, readings so many placards, and walking around the pool where Snorri was treacherously murdered we got back into the Getz and traveled on.

Despite the rain the sheep were as docile as ever as they wandered all about the fields occasionally blocking traffic and sending a bleat in our direction. The rain began to lift as we began exploring the lava fields and waterfalls of Hraunfossar, a large park area situated not far from Reykholt. The blues of the main waterfall were astonishing and we hiked all over the area bounding over rocks and water and finding Alice in Wonderland-like red topped mushrooms nestled between alien shrubbery.

Enjoying the peace of going off script for a bit, we decided to drive through a fjord in the countryside. For most of the late morning to early afternoon we talked about the joys of traveling, the things we had already seen and the myriad adventures which lie ahead. The sheep watched as our small yet reliable car wound along wet roads through tiny villages showcasing intact whale skeletons and other oddities. In the end we wound up in Akranes, a small town at the edge of the ocean with beautiful lighthouses and a wonderful small-town vibe. We ate lunch at a hippie cafe which doubled as a novelty shop full of Icelandic clocks with gnomes carved into the sides and artisanal cakes and coffees.

After talking with the barista for a bit we decided it best to head back to Reykjavik, luckily a beautiful drive along the coast. We gave back the trusty Getz to the rental agency and hauled our luggage to our new hostel in the center of town. Unlike before, Reed and I opened the door to our eight bed room and it was empty. Feeling rejuvenated we locked up our bags and went out in search of food and beer. With light diminishing we quickly found a restaurant serving traditional Icelandic soup inside a bread bowl with a light lager. The soup warmed us and our conversation soon turned to craft beer and the hunt was on. Our trusty itinerary listed a few local breweries and we were eager to hunt them down and we soon found ourselves in the basement of one of them with copper fermentation tanks to our backs and a cold beer to whet our lips.

From there we crawled to another fancy brewery and talked about what we had seen over the course of what felt like a week but in actuality was only two days. I'm pretty sure I hadn't stopped smiling since I boarded the plane in New York, it was ridiculous, it was like I was a child in the world's largest candy store where everything I could dream of was up for grabs. As the beer found its way down my throat my smile widened and the urge for more was greater.

We left the brewery and went for a walk down to the docks, around the downtown area, past a mailbox designated for children to drop off their Christmas wishlists, and into the tourist section of the city. It was getting late and our flight was at 7:30 the next morning but we decided it was worth it for one more beer; it was a vacation after all.

The establishment was called the American Bar and, as the name heavily implies, it was full of tourists mostly Americans. We sat at the bar next to a middle aged couple from Montana, the kind of tourists who had never left the country and decided after all these years to visit a place that was middle of the road, not too crazy but still within their comfort zone. The four of us talked for a couple hours, drank beers, talked about our pasts and futures and got told how lucky we were to do this kind of traveling while we are young.

More beers were pushed our way as midnight came and went. By this point Reed and I were looking over maps on our phones trying to figure out our path across Scandinavia. For months he had been asking me what I wanted to see and where I wanted to go? Each question was answered the same, "I don't want to plan anything. I just want to go wherever we want to go!" It must have been frustrating for him to have planned out Iceland like he did, which was extremely nice for the first country, but to have no idea what came next. We knew we would be flying to Helsinki in a few hours but besides that nothing was planned.

More beers came. It was approaching two in the morning and we were still pouring over maps only by this point we were talking about slipping into Russia.

"I've heard somewhere that American's can be in Russia for up to 72 hours before we need a visa!"

"Yeah, but I've heard they won't let you in without a fixer!"

The plan was to get to Helsinki in a few hours then book a flight to St. Petersburg and wing it from there. After however many beers we had had it sounded like a solid plan.

We left the bar around four in the morning and somehow bought more beer on the way back to the hostel. Drunk, we slowly opened the door to our room not wanting to wake anyone who may be inside. Once we gathered ourselves we came to the conclusion that we were alone, our room was empty! Ecstatic, we opened our beers and made a plan to stay up the entire night because what was the point in sleeping for a couple of hours anyway!

Our talking continued until about five when we simultaneously put down our beers and said to hell with it and crawled into our bunks. With my head reeling from countless pints of countless types of beer I looked at my phone and saw it was 5:30. Our plane would leave Iceland in two hours.

Chapter 3

Finland

With a shrill ring my phone alarm yelled at us telling it was 6:00 am. In a kind of drunken daze I rolled over in the stiff bunk digging my head in the pillow for my sleep when a shot of panic ran through my heart and I mumbled from somewhere deep within, "FUCK!!!"

My entire body shot of the bottom bunk and as I stood swaying I shook Reed and we both realized our plane would leave Iceland in an hour and a half.

In a kind of zombie state we mulled about our room rubbing our bloodshot eyes and grabbing miscellaneous items we had strung out from the night before. Each passing second shivered with anxiety as our brains became ever more aware of the predicament we had put ourselves in. Within minutes we had gathered our bags and left the hostel, hustling across damp grass and iced over snow piles until we reached the bus depot. At 6:30 we missed the bus and sat slightly slumped in the waiting area until a new bus approached ten minutes later. We lumbered onto the bus and were careening through the early morning darkness and, in what felt like ages, reached the airport.

With eyes burning and stomach churning we found ourselves at the back of a snaking line through security. Panicked, my bloodshot eyes scanned the area for a solution. There was no way we would make the flight if I had to check my gigantic bag, it was a fact. Then, on the wall next to the start of the security line, I saw a sign which read something like "oversized luggage." Since my pack was as big as I was I reasoned through my alcohol soaked brain that the sign must apply to my bag and my predicament.

Thinking myself a kind of genius I rushed over to the window and told the large, apathetic man behind the window what was happening, where I was going, and filled out a small tag which I watched him lace through a strap of my pack. The gigantic backpack was fed through a conveyor belt into the room which housed the oversized luggage and Reed, who by that point looked worse than I had ever seen him, and I rushed through security.

By some miracle we made it through the other side and were sitting at our terminal gate minutes before our flight was to depart. We boarded our flight to Helsinki and sat in our seats both feeling like death, the kind of feeling every adult has had when the body just wants, or needs, to sleep to rest to do something that doesn't include think or act in any way. Before we even took off Reed was sleeping next to me, mouth agape, while I watched out the window as we took off and left Iceland beneath us. I watched as the small portion of Iceland we had "conquered" slipped away into the clouds.

Before I had fed my large backpack through the conveyor belt I had made a day-pack, one which my mom, in her most pristine moment of over-preparedness, had made me take, filled with my camera, travel journal, extra pair of socks, undies, and shirt. As we flew higher and farther away from the first country of my European backpacking expedition I rested my head against the window. My alcohol ridden brain began to drift in-between past, present, and future in a dream-like state of exhaustion. Ever since I set foot on that train in Pasco my brain had been sharp and ready for whatever came its way. Now it was dull from lack of sleep, jet lag, travel, and an all night bender of who knows how many pints. On one hand I felt like an idiot but on the other, I felt like I had already made the first four days of my three month voyage worth it, every *single* minute. Everyone kept telling me to live this trip to its fullest, I was just living up to the advice countless people had given me, "Enjoy it, every second."

The plane landed, jolting us out of our restful sleep. Onto the baggage claim for the mundanity of waiting in lines and grabbing the bags that are always there amidst the others, except mine wasn't. Through the still-hungover haze I watched as people around me shuffled towards the conveyor belt to grab their bag that was always meant to be there. With every passing person my giant bag wasn't showing up and it wasn't until the conveyor belt made two complete passes when I and the other two women next to me hurried over to the help desk.

The blonde young woman behind the counter smiled and put on her best face and went through the pleasantries of a job which many people dismiss. After a few words and a couple distressed looks at her computer it was determined my bag was lost. Not 'lost in transit,' or 'it must be here somewhere, don't worry.' No, it was lost. Gone. Completely 'you are screwed,' fucking GONE.

In her most positive, scripted tone the attendant broke the news to me and my gut dropped. There was so much in that backpack, so many *essentials* I couldn't continue the trip without. Through my red, itchy eyes tears began to swell only to be pushed back by my thoughts of Reed sitting off behind me somewhere, I couldn't let him see me cry out of exhaustion and distress. I gathered myself and filled out the contact sheet and was told the airline had two weeks to search for the missing luggage until it turned into an insurance issue. The woman asked me where I would be in two weeks and all I could say was "I have no idea." The entirety of my plan was to not have an itinerary and at that moment in the Helsinki airport I began to regret every bit of my idiocy.

Composing myself, I walked back over to my zombie-like companion sitting, no slumped, on a bench near the baggage claim exit looking exhausted, on the verge of haggard. At his feet was the bag I had used as my carry on, the small day-hiking backpack looked insignificant, infinitesimally small. It was was all I had for thousands of miles. All I could think of was the old George Strait song "everything that I got, is just what I got on." A sense of pride welled up within me, this first set back, a rather major one, had taken place and I rambled my way through it. As we walked out into that Finnish sunlight of morning I felt like a kind of vagabond from a different time, little luggage on my back and an open, directionless road stretching long ahead of me.

After a short bus ride through the city, Reed and I made our way to our hostel, a large stadium originally built and used for the 1952 Helsinki Olympic Games. The outside was so impressive in its scale and history but once we entered the illusion faltered and we were met with a run down ruin of bygone glory days. Our room was an open square with bunk beds lining the walls and large hairy men with harsh sounding accents strutting about in various states of dress, hacking and spitting from all around. Exhausted from the night before and thankful to have a place to stay, we secured our bags, mine much easier now that it was a fraction of the weight and size, and were back into the sunshine and fresh air.

Helsinki felt much more open than Reykjavik and the buildings had a kind of Russian feel to them with the way the roofs were shaped and the amount of no nonsense straight lines fitted into the architecture. We wove in and out of residential streets, bought a few toiletries from a local market, and found ourselves standing at the docks looking out over a large sailing ship as the ocean stretched out in front of us. The night ended fairly early back at the Stadium Hostel with large men snoring in a kind of hellacious synchronicity which kept me awake most of the night.

Morning came with rain and breakfast planning in the hostel over black coffee. Neither of us cared much for the dormitory but due to my bag being lost and my inflated sense of hope at it getting found and shipped to me quickly we decided to stay another night. The rain soon turned into sunshine and we were out into the streets once again first visiting a couple of churches, then down into a large outdoor market along the water, and finally on a boat crossing the bay and landing on Suomenlinna, an island fortress built to defend the city a few hundred years ago.

With stone walls reaching toward all corners of the large island and with canons dotting certain vantage points, the fortress still seemed like it could ward off a modern day attack. The green grass was well maintained and people sat on the naked rocks watching as the waves rolled and many small boats passed with glorious sails bouncing lushes sun rays off their gleaming skins. For a piece of land built to defend against an invasion the atmosphere in the current day was relaxing and calm.

Reed and I wandered all around talking about how amazing it was to be in a country so far away. We talked about how close we were to Russia and brought up our drunken talk of flying to St. Petersburg and how amazing it was that we could literally travel anywhere in the world at a moments notice. As so many of our discussions reveal, the human experience is one of immense freedom, either the pursuit *of* it or the anxiety of realizing we have it only to then choose what to do with that knowledge. In our case on that island it was one of living in a moment where freedom was everywhere and we were to make the best of it.

After a few hours we ferried back to the docks of Helsinki and found a high-brow brewery. We paid the outrageous prices for the pints and talked with the bartender about topics we as craft beer bartenders would talk about in our outrageously pedantic way. Before long I realized how similar we all were and how even a few thousand miles of distance and vastly different cultures couldn't keep us from being similar.

On the way back to our hostel we stopped at a cathedral made of rock seemingly in the middle of the city. The atmosphere was dark as the only lights were hundreds of candles lining the walls of the cavernous room. Dark stained pews and worshippers with heads hanging filled the center as we stood in the back of the church observing. Minutes seemed to extend past their normal parameters as the atmosphere overtook my senses and I became engrossed in the rite. I think of myself as quite non-religious but in those moments it was pleasant to be amongst the initiated and feel the sanctity of the space surrounding us. I left that stone church feeling more at ease as we made our way back through the night.

The morning came with ease as we were up early and rushing to meet our train. Our next stop was the small harbor town of Turku. Our train barreled through the changing landscape of autumn with its green and red leaves lining the shores of blue water stretching out only interrupted by rocky islands. Reed and I both put headphones in and tuned out the world around us for the three hour ride, it felt nice to be alone on the rocking train. Blissful was the lack of noise.

It was late morning when we departed the train and made the short trek to our new hostel, a large ship bearing the name S/S Borea. A large ferry-style ship built in 1960, the Borea had been repurposed as a boat hostel and as we scaled the gangplank my boyish sense of adventure swelled to new heights. The interior of the ship was furnished with green carpet, dark stained wood trim and paneling, and the door ways were the watertight steel ovals so commonly seen in old nautical movies. After a quick check-in we wound through the ship and found our cabins. Unlike the Stadium Hostel in Helsinki, we each had our own personal cabin, quite small but private and each had a small port hole overlooking the small city.

With a renewed sense of vigor we exited the ship and soon found Turku Castle, a medieval castle which is one of the oldest structures in the country. We walked through the courtyard and admired the white walls and medieval architecture of the castle before strolling over to the Turku Cathedral. After a quick glance inside we bought some ice cream from a vendor and walked across an open square getting many looks from passersby but not thinking much of it. The main shopping district was filled with trinkets and clothes way out of our price range so we walked back to the square to find some food.

A small, blue building had pictures of every kind of hamburger combination imaginable plastered to each side of its walls. Every establishment we had gone before had been staffed with people who spoke excellent English and we had not encountered much in the way of language barriers; except then. Once confident in our decisions, we stepped toward the sliding window and were greeted by an old, hunched woman who spoke absolutely no English. Through a series of poor hand signals and an exchange of money we were assured through an overexcited series of head nods that our food was being prepared. As we stood waiting, a few rough looking guys got closer to us speaking to one another then nodding our direction, I didn't think we were being threatened but it definitely felt like we were outsiders who didn't belong in the square.

After some time the little old lady threw open her window and presented the burgers and fries we believed we had ordered. Thanking her in the Finnish "Quitos" we strolled across the open square biting into the burgers. A few bites in, we were sure it wasn't any kind of beef we were eating and later we were told it could have been reindeer, a common meat used in those kinds of settings. Regardless of the kind of meat, the burgers were gone before we left the square in search of something to wash them down.

With darkness about to fall we began climbing a hill toward an ominous looking building surrounded by a tall barbed wire fence. The looming building gave off an insidious vibe as we walked the perimeter guessing at all the secrets which could lie behind its walls. Once at the highest point we looked down on the lights of Turku and how they contrasted with the blank darkness of the ocean where we would not only lay our heads that night on her shore but trek into the following morning.

We arrived back to our boat hostel with a few cans of fruity local beer from a small market. Sitting in the dark at the wooden bar, empty of patrons and beaming with history, we talked about the next days journey to Sweden and our love of boats and water. Reed told stories of his youth and pubescence in Florida and how he owned a small boat which he would use to ferry friends to the Keys and swamp lands of the state. I mixed in stories from my summer of working on a commercial fishing boat in southeast Alaska and told of the people I had met and the waves we had encountered. The cold beers went down smooth in that bar on our final night in Finland. Acting much more responsible than in Iceland, we finished our beers before eleven and retired back to our cabins.

    As I crawled onto that hard mattress I looked up at the slanting roof illuminated from the glow of the city through the port hole and smiled at these little idiosyncrasies which makes every journey personal and unique. Although the boat was stationary my tired mind reminisced about how the Alaskan boat rocked at night in the various spots we docked and anchored and it soothed me in the way the water always has.

    Reed and I met for breakfast the next morning in the ship's dining hall, preparing ourselves for the voyage ahead. We walked through the heavy rain and dark clouds to the main shipping harbor of Turku where our modern day ferry was tethered waiting to undertake the long voyage across the open waters to Sweden. Everything went smoothly at check-in and we sat waiting amidst an eclectic group of travelers from a variety of different regions of the world each with their own accents being admitted into the atmosphere into a cacophony of clashing accents, cries and screams from young children tired from the hour, and vivacious family members saying their goodbyes to the ones they loved. Boarding was quick and before long the giant red ship broke away from the harbor and we were steaming out, starting the 11 hour voyage.

As was our custom, we quickly set out to explore our surroundings with the obvious first stop being the highest point possible. We wound through the throng of people clustered into small groups standing against windows and walked out onto the middle deck amidst a flurry of intense wind and spitting rain. Smiling, I hurried up a wet set of stairs and found a wide open top deck with a howling wind and fog on all sides of us. Reed soon reached me and we laughed and smiled at the storm we were going into. The only other person on the drenched deck was a young woman, about our age, named Petra from the Czech Republic. We introduced ourselves and decided it best to head back into the warmth of the ferry for some coffee.

Finding an open table the three of us sat down with our drinks and began to talk. Petra was in her late twenties with short brown hair and a cute face with eyes which showed kindness but also intensity. She had been traveling by herself up from her small town in the Czech Republic, visiting both Poland and Estonia, ferried across to Helsinki, and had gotten to Turku just in time to catch the ferry to Stockholm where she was planning to spend a few days before catching a flight back home. Reed and I told her about our trip so far and what we had tentatively planned over the next few days.

It was amazing how easy she was to talk to, within minutes it had seemed like I had known her for years. We talked about our interests and where we came from, compared our upbringings and how we saw the future. For a few hours the three of us talked and walked around the large ferry admiring its bars, slot machines, food courts, and numerous areas to buy random things.

At one point in the journey the ship began to rock with such an intensity that people had to sit down on the floor in order to regain their composure while the food court had to close due to soups and other food stuffs spilling out of their containers. Amidst the chaos the fisherman in me took over and I rushed to the top deck and was met by a howling wind and pouring rain. With a maniacal smile on my face I struggled to the stern-most rail of the struggling behemoth and stretched my arms and legs wide yelling into the storm. With my long hair and flannel shirt flapping in the wind, I closed my eyes and felt an all encompassing sense of awe come over me. It was at that point I realized where exactly I was and I *was* in the *moment*. I was truly present soaking up every second as it passed, not thinking about how I had gotten there or where I was going afterwards. I was the only person on the planet and all that mattered were those glistening moments stretching out into infinity. I felt all powerful not only for those moments but, more broadly, because I was doing *exactly* what I was supposed to do in my life at exactly the right time.

Many seconds passed as the ship rocked back and forth, my muscles reverting back to what they had learned on a much smaller boat in waters as rough as this in a place many thousands of miles away. I opened my eyes which were beaming out into that foggy abyss and I walked back to my two cold friends watching me with their intense eyes. We descended back into the ferry and after another hour Petra wanted to spend the rest of the voyage alone. Contact information was exchanged and a few last words of thanks were spoken and I watched her walk to a table facing the water and pull out a book. It is always amazing meeting people that are truly independent and are as happy in their heads as they are amongst a group of people.

Reed and I bought a few refreshments from a market brave enough to be open during those times of turbulent seas and we retired to a table at the bow of the ferry in a room designed for entertainment. Reed spent the remaining hours with his nose in a book written by Snorri Sturluson about Icelandic life many hundreds of years ago while I jotted notes from our experiences so far with the hopes of putting them to use some day.

With an announcement over the intercom we were entering the final leg of the voyage. We went back up to the top deck and watched as many small islands poked their way through the diminishing fog. Some islands had a lone cabin built on them while others had houses with neighboring windmills while still others had houses with saunas and a dock with a small boat attached. The islands began to come with trees and soon we were met with the sun setting and the city of Stockholm coming into view.

As our giant ferry slowly made its way toward its docking station Reed and I leaned against the railing and took it all in, the city was beautiful from the top deck of a ship many stories high. The ferry came to a shuttering halt as we bumped into the dock. With the excitement of a new country we descended into the ferry and joined the masses of voyagers waiting to be released upon the new city, the city of Stockholm.

Chapter 4

Sweden Pt. 1

With darkness not far away, Reed and I hurried along the waterway and into the business of Stockholm on a Saturday night. Along crowded streets and down into even busier underground systems we fought our way to the large arena situated just outside the downtown area of the city. As we tried exiting the underground, a swarm of people were making their way down into the tunnels blocking us off from the world above. We stood along the wall as hundreds of people squeezed through the turnstiles and pushed their way onto the escalators. Biding our time we finally found a hole in the swarm and pushed our way through into the streets only to be met with more people in a steady stream coming from the arena that was our home for the night.

The crowd turned out to be U2 fans erupting from the sold out arena. With much avoidance we eventually entered the now empty arena and made our way to the American-style bar housed underneath the stage made to look like a stereotypical sports bar a person might find on the east coast of the US. Confidently walking to the bar, we asked the bartender for directions on how to get to our hostel. With a look of "oh, so you don't now" on his face, the nice man showed us out into the hallway to a row of Sleep Capsules. Within a few moments he showed us how to work the new-age hostels which were the size of most standard closets. With key cards in hand, Reed and I stood at the opening of our capsule and smiled at how ridiculously small it was.

Making the best of the situation, I claimed the top bunk and crawled into it while Reed sat on the bottom bunk. For all intents and purposes it was cozy and would definitely suffice for the night. Without much entertainment we left our small sleep pods and went in search of beer. A gas station was close and we grabbed a couple of low alcohol lagers, the standard it seemed in Scandinavia after dark, and brought them back to the arena. As part of the hostel's, see broom cupboard, amenities a corner of the hallway, the same hallway bar patrons would traverse to use the restroom, was fitted with a couple of lawn chairs and a table. Not thinking ourselves too fancy for the situation, we sat in the corner and drank our beers laughing at the absurdity of it all. If I had been alone and been surprised with the Sleep Capsules I would have been all out of whack but with a travel companion, especially one with as relaxed demeanor as Reed, it was easy to let the unwelcome surprise turn to a situation of learning and laughter.

Stockholm met us with gray clouds as we emerged from our sleep pods and left the arena on our way to the medieval district of Gamla Stan. As we walked along the pastel colored buildings with their sharp features and dark-pointed roofs we joked about our strange sleeping arrangements and betted on the fact that they probably wouldn't be beat as far as "interesting hostels" was concerned. The rain was coming down quite intensely and made the few people meandering through the medieval district with their characteristically northern European dark clothes and straight faces seem hard yet charming and welcoming. I couldn't help but notice the attractiveness of all those around us. The young women with their blonde hair and tight-fitting black outfits held hands with tall, blonde, sharp-jawed partners in equally tight trousers and they walked down the sidewalks like it was a sopping wet catwalk and we were the commoners set to gaze at their dashing good looks. These couples were everywhere and it was difficult not to take notice of them and their looks and the confidence radiating from their taught cores.

 We walked the cobbled streets of the medieval district, winding around black iron-topped buildings with sharp spires and shops tucked into nooks with throngs of tourists eating and gazing in every window. The rain subsided and we trudged on and on until we found ourselves in a residential area across one of the many bridges from the central area which gave a fine view of the Gamla Stan. Following brightly colored graffiti, we stood atop a large rock and watched the small people walk around and stare at the medieval buildings as the river gently rolled along underneath the skies with clouds parting and a warm Swedish sun soaking us with rays which did their best to push away the rainy gloom of that late September day. There is much to be said of getting away from the tourist traps and heady architecture of a beautiful city and reaching out into the faceless residential areas and seeing what the locals experience in their everyday lives.

    The rest of that beautiful sunlight was spent walking along the river and back through the cities innards until we found a theme park area. Not wanting to pay the entrance fee we watched from afar at the tall rides and classic feel of the place until we became hungry and found ourselves at a tightly packed brewery along a cobble stoned street. The brewery was absolutely amazing with their selection of sour beers and stouts with pizza and calzones and a young crowd beaming with energy and excitement which can only happen when like minded people get together in a tight group and imbibe in the elixirs that make us truly human, intoxicants of your choosing.

    My companion and I relished in the beauty of the brew and had pint after pint with our conversation reaching peaks of liveliness and our plans of the future more grandiose. Our time together had already passed the halfway point but it didn't matter, not that night, what mattered was where we were. Back in America, nestled in the middle of rural Oregon drinking beers in the middle of a thousand acre hop farm we dreamt about nights like that, could have only dreamt because the actual experience at that brewery in Stockholm was the epitome of what I believe travel to be, a true experience no amount of money or tour guides could give.

After a few hours we emerged from our beer haven and took in the night's air crisp and cool with a bit of salt from the ocean just there in the blackness of night. The cobble stones felt proper instead of awkward and the buildings all around us felt familiar as we walked down toward the docks to board our hostel for the night. Our boat hostel was similar to the one we stayed in back in Finland only much smaller and better kept. With the buzz of the brewery still floating our heads, we dropped our bags in the small cabin, this time having to share a space, and ascended to the top deck of the boat. Opening the hatch we walked out onto the deck to crisscrossing strands of large bulbed lights casting a warm glow between the boat's smokestacks and a magnificent view of the city of Stockholm at night with its lights sparkling in the distance.

Conversation ensued as we sat in the lounge chairs talking about our travels and how lucky we were to have actually done such an amazing trip. We talked of beers and the sights we had seen, the beauty of the Swedish girls in their short black skirts, and the history of the area and how little we knew about what we were surrounded by. The hour turned late and we found our way back to the small cabin we were to call home for the night. Like usual I climbed to the top bunk and the lights went out and my brain was buzzing, not from the alcohol, but from the pure joy and realization that we were truly present, truly in the moment, living every second and not letting even one go to waste. It was a mindset I had hoped I would find along this trip and it was one that I was lucky enough to experience every day.

Chapter 5

Norway

Sleeping on an old boat is charming during the day and even exciting at night but once the morning comes reality sets in and I understood why the seaman of old didn't care to live aboard a boat if they could avoid it. Our cabin was interesting because it was essentially one room which was divided into two. One side was a cramped placement of a small bunk bed with an even smaller chest-of-drawers to its side while the other side of the room was a small toilet, an even smaller sink, and a shower head. These two sides were separated by a plastic curtain and not much else.

Reed was the first to shower while I looked up train routes to get to our next destination and what there was to do once we were there. After he was finished I hopped down from the top bunk onto a soggy floor. Not thinking much of it I ducked into the shower area to find everything sopping wet. Water was dripping from the sink and toilet while the walls glistened with droplets. As fast as I could I showered causing more water to fly all around the small enclosure and leaking out toward the bunk beds. We left the small cabin not long after and laughed at how it felt like it had gotten steadily smaller since we first saw it the night before.

We boarded our train and set-off through the woody countryside which would be our backdrop for the next six hours. By this point in the trip Reed and I had spent an obscene amount of time together. We were companions on an endeavor with our comfort zones completely blasted apart and we relied heavily on one another for companionship but also for daily sanity. Because of this, we had spent every hour together and as soon as the train began rolling we each, silently and without a word being said, reached into our bags, pulled out our headphones, and tuned out the world. For six hours we were in our own worlds as the world moved around us. Once the train arrived at the Oslo station I felt recharged and ready to tackle whatever the new country had to offer.

It was early afternoon and we emerged from the station onto a busy plaza with many people sitting on large steps smoking and talking and bustling in a general way. The night before we had talked about reserving a hostel but decided not to and chance it. We had reserved all of our hostels at least twenty-four hours in advance up until that point and our expertise at traveling Europe was at an all time high, why not throw a bit of spontaneity into the mix?

This notion came crashing down when we stood there, baggage in hand, scouring through our repertoire of hostel booking apps and websites only to find that everything was booked. With a bit of worry, we walked to a cheap hostel only a few blocks from the train station and, after wading through a gaggle of backpackers, found the front office and were quickly told there was nothing available and that we would have quite a difficult time finding any room at such short notice. We were back on the street not far from where we had started but an hour later and with night not caring about our predicament.

Again, we searched all over the internet for any kind of room within our budget but the only available rooms were fancy hotels way out of our price range. By some kind of miracle, as the skies became gray and night encroached Reed found a cheap, slightly sketchy hotel in a questionable neighborhood that was taking lodgers. Ecstatic, we lugged our bags a couple miles through wonderfully kept streets with gorgeous buildings and expensive cars, past a wreck scene where two city trams collided crunching the front of one and the back of the other, and finally into a residential area which had seen better days when we finally reached our shady hotel.

Checking-in we were beyond grateful to not have to face the alternative and found our room, about four times the size of our boat cabin, and went in search of beer. Norway, like all of Scandinavia, has a ridiculously high tax on its alcohol and also regulates the strength of that alcohol once the sun sets. With our standards quite low, we found a gas station nearby and bought whatever liquid they labeled as beer and brought it back to our room. The beer was awful, especially after the grand experience we had the night before at the Stockholm brewery but it didn't matter. After that kind of day and that kind of stress lying in a firm bed with a cold beer brought everything back to neutral. The night was still young and there was an inkling desire to explore the night but we both agreed it best to turn in early and the lights went out.

Morning came with blue skies and a renewed sense of wonder and energy as we quickly gathered our things and jetted out the door ready to see Oslo in the stressless joy of of a new day. The streets of the city were bustling and alive with blue skies and a crispness of late autumn in the air. It was early and the vendors were only just putting their sandwich boards on the streets while starry-eyed tourists opened secure hotel doors and walked smiling into the streets ready for the day.

Before long we were walking along the marina and into a line of people waiting to board one of the many boats going out to the group of islands which make up the archipelago branching off from mainland Norway. The map next to the ticket office had dashed lines darting in every direction from where our line stood and without much thought we chose an island, boarded a boat a few minutes later, and were soon cruising swiftly along the water in the morning sun.

There weren't many of us aboard the boat so when we reached the docks to the rocky island we dispersed on our own and walked along a trail lined with a thin smattering of trees. It felt nice to get away from the bustle of a city environment and get into nature, no matter how contained. Reed and I had spent many hours hiking along remote Oregon trails over the months we had been friends, using those wanderings as a time to talk about weird topics he and I found interesting and others didn't seem to. We talked about the brewery he dreamed of opening with his long-term girlfriend, the books I wanted to write, the forms of art we both enjoyed, and the places in the world we hoped to see before we became unable. The rugged environment of that island in Norway brought out the same topics only much more present. Our time in Europe together was coming to a close and we each felt it. As we walked through the trees, across boulders, and down to the water line the day's warmth pushed away any feelings of sadness. We were living that day as we had all of the others, to its fullest and most complete.

We were on the island for a few hours but once our stomachs began to growl we made our way to the docks and set forth back to the marina of Oslo. After an unremarkable lunch, we took a city bus to a complex housing the Oslo Viking Ship Museum and were amazed at what lie within. As usual, I hadn't done any kind of research before visiting the site so when we walked in and a fully intact Viking warship spread out in front of me I couldn't help but smile the same kind of smile which had become commonplace amidst all the amazing sites we had seen along the trip thus far.

The wood of the ship was an extremely dark brown, bordering black, with intricate carvings and markings beautifully decorating different parts of the ship. Situated away from the main ship were various Viking exhibits excavated from the same site as the main ship and from varying sites from all over the Norwegian countryside. Each piece was carefully constructed with a craftsmanship I had not expected from my preconceived, and false, notion of the Vikings as murderers and pillagers who took what they needed from others and didn't have the desire to make lasting things of their own.

In actuality that myth of the Vikings is just that, a falsely held belief perpetuated by generations of misleading information. Walking out of that museum left me with an entirely different view of a group of people the Norwegians, and the rest of Scandinavia, look at with cultural pride. It seems the more information archaeologists gather about the Vikings the more impressive they become. A short walk away from the Viking Ship Museum was another museum which was a full-sized replica of a Viking village. With the same kind of almost-black wood used for construction, the buildings were large and sturdy, built to last through the centuries and endure the frigid atmosphere of northern Europe.

The complex was almost completely devoid of people as we wandered in and out of the various, extremely well constructed replicas. One was a bunkhouse, another a kitchen, one a barracks, all with the capacity to instantly remove the outside world and transport us back to a time very long ago. We walked along the dirt road past what would have housed their livestock and after a few grassy bends came to an open field with a stave church situated in the middle. The church was quite tall and thin with the characteristic almost-black wood rising in sharp triangles to the point adorned with fierce, wooden gargoyles jutting out from each of the four corners making up the roof. Upon first sight it looked to be a piece of art and not a building once used to house actual people in times of worship. As we walked closer the intricacy of the church all but demanded attention with its dominance making me feel the gravity of its symbolism and importance. The people who built it took great pride in their handiwork and must have felt a deep connection and duty in their work from the larger pieces to the small, even the door was intricate and divine. We walked along the outside of the beautiful building taking in the size and presence and I was overwhelmed with thoughts of the many people from the past who would must have visited the church whether to engage in a kind of worship or to stand in awe at the work of the hands of mortal men acting in the aura of the divine.

Rain began to drizzle over us and the few tourists surrounding the stave church so we retraced our steps away from the church, through the village, and back to the bus stop in front of the Viking ships. Attempting to escape the rain, we ducked into a large area packed with people and with a dozen or more food and beverage vendors. Meandering through the hundreds of people we settled on a small bar for beer and food and talked of the day's journey. Neither of us were expecting to be hit so hard by history and I couldn't help but be impressed by Reed's ability to find such extraordinary places throughout Scandinavia.

After lunch we found our way to a brewery near the center of the city. The beers were quite good but Norway's alcohol tax made them expensive and made me worry about money and how much I had already spent in the short time with Reed. I had saved nearly $7000 from my time working within the hop farm's pub and was not entirely sure it would be enough to cover all of the three month endeavor I had rather hastily embarked. Reminding myself with every purchase to spend less and watch my spending I was in a state of constant monetary dread with each passing day. Failure was defined as having to cut the three month trip short and skulk home to live with my mom, failure would be a knowledge that I couldn't live cheaply enough to make it the entire way, simply put, failure just wasn't going to happen.

Shaking off the anxiety we talked of our plans for tomorrow and how to make it back to Sweden. As we were leaving a Norwegian man at the door, the bouncer, made small talk with us and we asked him about places to see before we left the country. Without hesitation he told us to go to the old Olympic stadium and see the amazing views of the city from high atop a hilltop. We thanked him and wandered through the city and back to our hostel.

We hadn't realized how early it was and feeling good from the beers and the day we had had we set off into the night without much of an idea of where we were heading. Within minutes we found ourselves in a large park, decently lit with a long walkway leading to an ornate fountain in the center. Lost in conversation, we walked along the path but soon noticed the green, life-sized statues lining the walkway. Each statue depicted a different version of a man or a woman. Some were dancing, some had children, others held each other tight, and some were in inhuman positions. There were dozens of them along the walk and once we passed the fountain, held up by *more* human statues, we came to an exhibit of mammoth proportions.

In the center of a raised complex of circular steps was an obelisk of cement or stone people in a huddled, faceless mass. From that central point there were groups of larger-than-human sized statues depicting different stages of human life. There was one group with babies, others with males and females courting, and another with old and feeble statues in the later stages of life. Reed and I walked around the complex numerous times taking in this gigantic art installation which we were not expecting to see and trying to make sense of it all. We spent maybe an hour looking and talking and sitting and talking and watching as random people would come up to the complex in the darkness and do as we were doing only to leave with questioning faces.

I left the complex feeling confused in the best possible way. It's not every night a person can walk out into the night only to come across a massive art installation which unfolds into a culmination of the existence of man. When my head hit my pillow in the darkness of our room the ambiguous faces of those statues ran through my head and I thought of that obelisk with its faceless masses crunched together jutting to the heavens. The day was finished and the next day begun, only to repeat itself on and on and on.

After a night filled with thoughts of faceless statues I woke to glorious Norwegian blue skies once again and hurried out the door in search of height. Following the instructions from our bar bouncer friend from the night previous, we took a public transport train out of Oslo proper and climbed to Holmenkollen National Arena, the sight of a large ski jump which had been home to ski competitions since the late nineteenth century.

Departing the train we trekked up to the ski jump, devoid of tourists, and walked around with images of airborne Scandinavians filling our heads. The imposing ski jump was by far the most eye-catching attraction in the complex even more than a picturesque chapel situated next to a pond, the same chapel which had been razed by death metal arsonists in 1992 but rebuilt a few years later, and a shotty view of the city of Oslo, a far cry from the views we were promised by our bar bouncer friend.

As we stood looking at the less-than-amazing view of the city a gaggle of women on elongated roller skates and ski poles cruised by training for cross-country skiing. They didn't seem to even acknowledge us as I found myself staring in wonder at the amount of effort it must have taken to skate up and down the monstrous hills we had surmounted by rail only an hour before. Unwilling to accept the view of Oslo as a complete loss, we ducked into a thicket of trees in hopes of climbing higher for the spectacular view but were soon greeted by a large statue of a gnome and a confirmed closure to the sites we were promised.

We walked back to the train stop talking about gnomes and what we knew of them from scraps of mythology which turned into talks of Reed's favorite film director Werner Herzog and a film he made about ski jumping which turned into talks of how he had met the acclaimed director outside a restroom and the talks turned into art and where we were going next until the train screeched to a stop and we, the only two people around, walked on board to continue talking about what we found interesting. Our bags were already packed so when we reached the central station of Oslo in a short time we boarded a real train and said goodbye to Norway and rode the rails east back to Sweden.

Our time in Norway was short, less than 48 hours, but memorable and well worth the trip. The train sped across wild country glistening with gorgeous weather and we both vowed to come back to the incredibly diverse landscape of Norway of which we had seen but a slight sliver. The hands of our clocks were not to rest as Sweden beckoned again.

Chapter 6

Sweden Pt. 2

The train from Norway came to a stop in Gothenburg, a relatively large city on the western coast of Sweden. With shoulders aching from a morning of carrying our packs, Reed and I departed the station without any idea of where we were headed. Exhausted, we stopped after a few minutes at a small, vacant cafe and ordered coffees and sandwiches, tapped into their WiFi, and tried to catch our bearings.

One of the main drawbacks to speedy travel is the head spinning. Changing sleeping establishments each night and having to navigate a new city every other day is amazing and is something both I and my companion enjoyed but every once in awhile a perfect concoction of exhaustion, lack of food, and a navigational malaise sets in and the only cure is to physically sit down and think. The cafe energized us in the best way and after our foodstuffs were consumed we walked into the streets with a purpose and a hostel in our sights.

Gothenburg is a college town and like the majority of cities devoting themselves to that endeavor there is a certain *feel* that is almost palpable in the way the people hold themselves, converse, look, and do everyday things. Storefronts are a bit more arty and the citizens seem younger even though some haven't seen youth in many decades. As we walked to our hostel all of this surrounded us and it felt nice to be amongst it all, to soak up a different atmosphere, and to be around people who wouldn't think us foolish for choosing this kind of glorified homelessness so sought after among the dreamers of this lot.

After a couple miles of trudging we finally made it to our hostel, shitty even by the standards we had become accustomed but homey in the fact they had beds with our names on them. We dropped our packs and gave the bland establishment a once over before getting back on the streets. Dusk was nearing the skyline and we climbed a hill to a kind of fortress with a shimmering golden crown and took in the city from up high. Amazingly, the European beauty that was once unique and awe inspiring had become customary and glimmered in a familiar way.

We descended the hill and found a packed bar, ordered beers and sat next to the windows. The bar was lively and filled with Swedish college kids acting the exact same as college kids from anywhere else in the world. It was raucous and electric. Alcohol was traded for sensual looks from members of the opposite sex, or whatever sex was fancied, and the music was that perfect mixture of loud and calm and insightful and body swaying.

Reed and I got lost in the beer and the vibe and talked excitedly about what we had been through the past week and a half. We ordered more beer, and more, and more until my head was buzzing like that hum from a light bulb increasing in wattage. The bar's energy was increasing with the same frequency as my head and the lights became brighter and my speech faster. It was always hard to tell when Reed was feeling the effects of alcohol, he managed his buzz maybe the best I had ever seen, but I could tell he was feeling good.

Around midnight we left the bar and walked along the cobbled street to an English bar clearly built for tourists. Inside, the walls were literally covered with every possible knick-knack of stereotypical English memorabilia possible. The Swedish bartender welcomed us warmly with his charming accent and the only other person in the bar, an older man with a beer who had been in the middle of a drunken conversation with the bartender seconds before we walked in, looked at us with a smile. For the next two hours the four of us talked about all manner of things from Swedish culture, how fucked up America is, the beauty of Swedish women, compared beer between our countries, and the travels we had ahead of us. Beer was drank by all parties and the man behind the counter was generous with his time and patience as we consumed more beer, myself two American beers of all things, until leaving around three.

The walk back to our shitty hostel was glorious as the air smelled heavier and crisp and my head rang with clarity of what we were doing and where we were. People were still out on the streets, some in much worse states than ourselves, and all were living for the moment, doing what young people do in the light of the moon.

Morning came with a headache and a thirst for gallons of water. Gathering ourselves, we checked out of the hostel and found a cheap breakfast at a small cafe. Reed and I walked a bit trying to minimize the impact of our hangovers and the sunshine helped. We boarded the train midmorning and set-off south to our next destination, eyes closed in the soothing rocking of our carriage.

A few hours later we stepped off the train in Malmo, south of Gothenburg, and walked down to the waterfront. Ships loomed large as they were tied to the harbor resting from generations of work at sea and yearning to let out once again. The clouds were gray looking out past the harbor toward the ocean and a slight wind brought the familiar chill of impending winter to the coast of northern Europe. It would be bitterly cold in only a couple of months time.

We walked along the harbor, passed statues of Swedish seamen whose names were unknown to us, and still passed further beside ancient seafaring vessels which looked like something from the brain of Jules Verne including one diving apparatus which would have made his Captain Nemo quite content all those leagues under the sea.

The streets looked much the same as Stockholm and Gothenburg as we lazily strolled along the familiar architecture and past the political banners advertising Malmo as a safe-haven for refugees. It seemed to be the common thought among the Scandinavian countries to welcome the refugees and anyone who felt persecuted by their countries to find safe haven within their walls and assimilate into a culture ready to welcome all those who needed a helping hand. I found myself taken aback by the openness of these offers.

Before visiting, I had thought of Scandinavia as a rich culture who enjoyed their history but rather enjoyed their relative isolation from mainland Europe. Once on their soil and being immersed among them, I found the truth to be quite the opposite. The people to the north were welcoming and friendly to an infectious level, willing to help a person who is in need and politically a group who seek humanitarian goals founded on the most basic principles of neighborly generosity and an openness it seems many individuals, let alone entire countries, would be behooved to adopt. Reed and I discussed this on our way to the Malmo Castle, an establishment very much built on the opposite of these principles many generations ago.

Malmo castle is quite stunning with its red-tinted exterior and draw bridge spanning a straight-out-of-folklore moat. We stood within the courtyard and I looked down at the cobblestones and thought of the many thousands of feet which have stood right where I have, each pair thinking something different and in the castle for very different reasons. Without wanting to pay the tour fee we opted out of going inside the castle and continued on our blind trek through the city. Dusk was nearly upon us as we found our cheap hotel-hostel, checked-in, and soon found ourself at a drinking establishment indulging in the brewed beverages of Europe.

After a pint had gone down I started to become anxious. There was only one more country left on the Great

European Tour which included both Reed and I; in three days I would be alone.

    I tried to forget about the impending isolation by bringing up the beauty of the Swedish girls with their blonde hair and identical black mini skirts which soon led to conversations of Werner Herzog, Theodore Roosevelt, and stories of Reed's favorite concert composer who had spent a long winter alone in the northern tip of Norway to write a book and play music. We both smiled wide and talked about the novels I would write someday and the movies he would make and how we would travel to the tips of Norway together before we had kids and were married and long before the thrill of adventure ever left us. By the time the next pint touched my lips my anxiety was neatly buried in my brain but every so often I could hear the dull scratching and my head would turn slightly and I knew I would soon be alone.

Chapter 7

Denmark

The train arrived in the station with the clouds gray and full, a rain seemed imminent. Reed and I departed the metal snake which had twisted and weaved its way from Sweden, across bridges suspended above North Atlantic water, and into the sprawling train depot which was Copenhagen Central. The station was busy with people of all ethnicities scurrying in every possible direction while security guards stood at the ready with their bullet proof vests and faces full of apathy. Smiling at the thought of entering the last of our countries together I glanced at my companion and saw a determination and a confidence in his face which I would soon miss.

Once out under the gray clouds of mid-morning the air felt full and new. Cars were speeding by on the roads and pedestrians were hurrying along on their way to work or play or whatever, it was the middle of the week and there was no time to delay. Without hesitation we entered into the stream of people and were quickly swept along the sidewalk and into an open plaza with the City Hall of Copenhagen and all its glory standing tall above us. The square was full of tourists with a tremendous collection of maps and cameras and hands formed into peace signs. We gathered our bearings and walked toward our hostel.

As we had planned, the hostel was quite near the city center and within minutes the multi-story face of the hostel came into view along with the denizens sprawled lazily upon over-stuffed pillows and old couch cushions thrown carelessly along the sidewalk. These cheery patrons of the hostel had fists full of drinks and mouths full of cigarettes and smiles and ceaseless conversations full of laughter and perceived whimsy. There were cat calls and jeers from this group as we walked in what we would soon become aware was a party hostel.

One of our first clues alluding to the fact that the hostel wasn't merely a hostel was the fact that the check-in counter was the bar, a long, chic expanse with numerous taps and triple the amount of liquor bottles behind it along the mirrored bar-back. The man with tattooed forearms, gauged ears, and a "fuck you too" attitude met us, took our passports and checked us in. After he was through, careful not to break a smile, he offered us a drink then showed us to our room.

The room was a large one with five loud, metal bunkbeds scattered around it. Buried within two of the beds were young men who were sleeping soundly and snoring loudly, rustling from our entrance and providing an example of the decibel which the squeal of the beds could truly reach upon the slightest movement. Reed and I exchanged a look with each other then, like we had done for two weeks

,with the underwhelmed emotions that is hostel life, we found our own bunks, hid our stuff with a lessening care and exited the body odor and stale cheese smell of the men's dormitory.

    Before we left, we gave the hostel a once over. Until then, we had not stayed at a "party" hostel and I was curious what the difference, if any, was between it and a "normal" hostel. The bar was obviously stocked exceedingly well as was the proportion of attractive, seemingly single young men and women. There were numerous booths situated along the walls of the large square room which housed the bar as well as low ambient light and a pool table tucked into a corner. The downstairs area was full of games and seats and a smaller bar with a conglomeration of lights used, for what I assumed, were dance parties, or discos as was common to the European night life. As it was before noon on a weekday the downstairs was completely empty and the main lobby/bar had only a couple young guys at the bar getting the day started in what could only be described as adventurous.

    The patrons sprawled lazily upon the random assortment of cushions smiled widely as we exited their bar and a few raised their glasses to a new day, one in which they would only half-heartedly take part in. As for the two of us, we were filled with the excitement which can only come from exploring a new place. We walked back toward the City Hall and turned at a street which looked good, or looked like a main artery of sorts. Bicycles with cheery faced riders pedaled past at high speeds at great frequency some yelling an excited expression in Danish. Our heads swiveled constantly as we took in the architecture of the residential areas, the street art, fountains, and soon came to a bridge which had many people stopped pointing at the water. Deep within the murky green were statues, after a quick ask-around we found out they were a group of mermen waiting for someone to return home. They were beautifully cast and I looked at their faces and felt sadness and longing, I wondered how many people a day saw these statues and how many simply walked by without a passing notice?

We continued on along that canal past large buildings with intricate roofs, one with alligators and curling tails, past a church of some import then onto a bridge over a large body of water and down into an entirely new district of Copenhagen. This district, Nyhavn, was filled with sailing vessels of all kinds roped to the docks with brightly painted buildings behind them and diners enjoying their meals on the cobblestones. The area was inviting and we soon found ourselves walking along the cobblestones with a beer in our hand smiling and laughing at the simplicity of life and the things that make people happy.

As the afternoon turned to night we kept up our wandering and stood atop the bridge over the large body of water in silence and watched as the lights turned on. It was peaceful and calm. That is the marker of a true friend, where two people can stand in silence in an open space and feel completely embraced and satisfied. It is as if the universe cast a unique blanket over the occupants of that particular space and filled it with something more tangible than dark energy but less mushy than love, it is a warmth which can only be beaten by unconditional familial love like that of a child or the mother who gave birth to the person standing in that space.

The party hostel was in full swing as we returned. Instead of the cushion dwellers being the only life outside the building there were instead twice as many people standing as there were pillow loungers. We walked through the crowd of accents and peaked-out pheromones through the door of the hostel and went straight to the bar. Surprisingly, they had excellent beer on tap and Reed, being the beer connoisseur he is, found something which satisfied his experienced taste buds and I found something which would take the edge off a long day of traveling. The room which had earlier been empty with the exception of a few professional drinkers was now swollen with laughing faces attached to hands filled with a variety of elixirs which sparkled in the dim, ambient lighting. Reed and I found a booth in the corner and began jabbering on about serious jibber-jabber which we deemed to be important, few others shared in this sentiment.

As we were in the depths of something about Werner Herzog and his connection to filming something in the Amazon, three beautiful girls walked up to our table and sat down confidently, two next to Reed and one me. By that point I had had a couple of beers and the thousands of miles away from home testosterone kicked in fiercely and I began conversation. It turned out the girls were in their early twenties and were from Germany. As was the case with many young people along the trip, they were taking a kind of gap year away from school and responsibilities and decided to be different and travel to northern Europe instead of the typical sunny south. They were all blonde with green or blue eyes, the kind of eyes one only sees in a hostel. A kind of starry, anything-is-possible vibe mixed with a hippy wanderers empathy and courage. The five of us talked about all manner of things most of all where we had gone and what I was about to embark on alone.

After a solid hour of great conversation an awkwardness cast its dark shadow across our table. It felt like they were waiting for something, perhaps us to buy them drinks or to take them to a club or maybe something as simple as offering them a game of pool. Whatever the cause of the silence, Reed and I read it wrong and just like that the three cute girls from Germany walked off not to be seen by our eyes again.

"Would you?" I asked with a devious smile.

"Z— wouldn't mind if I did," he said. "I don't think it counts if I am this far away from her. But I probably wouldn't anyway."

It made me smile the way he felt about his long-term girlfriend. It made me miss my ex something fierce but also aroused in me a kind of conquest-inspired testosterone which made me wish I had stepped up in that moment of awkward silence with the German girls. It made me wish, if only for a second, that this trip had changed me in some way. Yet, in reality it only made stronger what was already there, and always had been, all the parts that made me *me* were only going to stretch and bend and like an exercised muscle become stronger. I think only a select few individuals can actually *change* from travel, the rest of us are lucky to experience feelings of enlightenment, self-worth, and motivation; all entities which I fully embraced.

The beers kept coming to our table as our conversation kept getting nerdier in the best possible way, the way only my best friend and I could accomplish. Midnight came and went and before long it was early morning and we climbed the numerous flight of stairs, passed many groping couples smelling of stale drink along the way, and finally opened the door to our all male dormitory. The familiar smells of body odor, sour breath, wet socks, and dankness permeated its way to our nostrils in a way only a hostel can. Sleep came easy but the missed opportunity, whatever that would have been, with the German girls lingered on through the night and plundered my dreams of complete serenity.

Morning came as it had for two weeks, snoring men scratching crevices of hairy body parts best left to the imagination. As I rolled over, my head ached from the constant drinking which had become a regularity for our trip. I stared up at the bars of the bunk above me and smiled at the new day, a bright one from the looks of the curtains across the room. Rolling to the edge of the bed, I tucked my long hair up underneath my stocking cap, pulled up my trousers and quietly tiptoed across the creaking floor and out of the door.

To my amazement Reed was sitting at one of the booths with a coffee and his enormous book of Scandinavian folklore written by Snorri. His blue eyes were bright despite the night of drinking and he looked fresh, I, on the other hand, felt the exact opposite. I waved away the offer of coffee and was soon treated to the complimentary breakfast the hosel provided. Those in line at the buffet looked much worse for wear than I felt and it made me perk up just a bit.

After breakfast, we left the hostel, passed the drunkards outside stretched across the pillows and walked on along the canals for a while until we came to a large statue and a man holding a bright red and white striped umbrella. Across the umbrella was written FREE WALKING TOUR and we huddled into the mass of people forming and within minutes were walking along the city streets of Copenhagen on a tour with a middle-aged English man which had lived in Copenhagen for twenty years. The man was amazing in so many ways. His knowledge of the city was immense, his sense of humor impeccable, and his *love* for what he did was incredible.

In our three hour tour we went to all of the major tourist locations of Copenhagen including the mermen statues, a church with a boat inside it, examined unique architecture, walked up and down canals, ventured into Nyhavn, walked along the woods above the city, visited the Little Mermaid statue, and finished with a tour of the drughaven that is known as Christiania, a free-state nestled in the middle of Copenhagen where drugs are looked over by law enforcement and are essentially legal to buy and sell. Walking through the drug area felt sketchy on many levels due to the numerous signs warning against taking photos and the masked figures of any drug dealer even attempting to sell whatever kind of drugs they were. In an attempt to keep us safe it felt as if a giant sign had been attached to our convoy of twenty or so tourists like a beacon to all the drug dealers who were looking to make an extra buck and equally so to the real dealers who wanted nothing to do with us.

 The tour ended on the outside of the gates of Christiania and we all tipped the amazing tour guide with whatever we could. Before departing many of us asked where to find food and he pointed majority of us to a warehouse nearby full of food trucks. At first I was skeptical but once we walked into the expansive building all doubt faded. As far as the eye could see there were food trucks of every nationality and cuisine stretched for what seemed like miles. Some places were selling traditional Italian food, others Hawaiian, some Danish food, while others were selling hot dogs. The smell of hand-made pasta clashed brilliantly with the sickly sweet aroma of freshly made caramel corn. Beer smells mixed with wines, while doughs mixed with spices. It was a Foodies heaven if I had ever saw one.

 Reed and I split up and I wandered throughout the labyrinthian complex that was the warehouse. After three or four laps of the place I finally settled on my meal, an authentic Greek gyro with pasta and greens accompanied by a craft IPA from a local brewery. I walked out into the fading sunlight amidst one of Copenhagen's many canals and found Reed already diving into a delicious dish of freshly baked pizza and beer. We sat and ate as the sun went down over Denmark and the canals and the talking people and the beautiful world in which we were so lucky to have lived that particular day.

Once our food was eaten and our beers were refilled we began discussing the tour from earlier and how much we both enjoyed it. A part of the tour, not intentional by any means on the part of the guide, wouldn't leave me. Somewhere in the middle of the tour a young Australian guy, maybe 22, skipped up next to Reed and I and struck up a conversation. The guy looked a little rough, scraggly hair, hadn't shaved in a few weeks, and his clothes were a bit grimy even dirty in some spots. The typical questions followed upon meeting, "where you guys from," "what brings you guys to Denmark," followed by a selfish diatribe of their own story they were too polite to spout off from the beginning. The difference with this guy wasn't in his questions, those were asked and answered jovially by all parties, but in his responses. Instead of him acknowledging our existence then quickly going into his own awesomeness he asked a simple question, "how?"

Reed was only a day away from returning back home so his stake in this masculinity game was nowhere near where mine was, "what do you mean, how?" I asked as if offended in the way I had conducted myself over the course of the past two weeks.

Upon the reception of that question the Australian guy smiled a smile which had such an extreme self-confidence in it my guard was let down and I felt my head move back. As we walked with the rest of the tour group he told me his story. As was established from his accent, and, later, his telling me, he was from Australia and was at the point in his life where he wasn't sure what he would do. Like so many of his peers, he had decided to venture off to areas of the world he had not yet seen and ended up in the southern part of Italy three months previous. Once he had arrived he got work at a vineyard, made some money and lived free, then ventured up to the north of Italy where he bought a motorcycle and crossed much of central Europe staying at flea-bag hostels which boasted the cheapest rent and saving every cent he could. The motorcycle gave out in Germany and he traded it in for a bicycle and pedaled the remaining distance to Copenhagen as fast as he could for the cheapest he could. When we met him he only had a few hundred dollars, Australian, in his bank account and not a clue where to go next or how he would get home when his open-ended conquest of Europe was complete.

 I stood there feeling like a capitalist pig listening to the guy speak. In the three months he had spent in Europe by the time we had met him he had spent about the same amount as I had in two weeks. Each day I was wondering and whining about the uncertainty of my own travels and how to find an appropriate balance between comfort and cost and here this guy was living the dream of everyone who ventures away from their home looking for adventure and he was spending a fraction of what I was without even trying.

 Appalled, I tell myself I was done living the beurgeoisie lifestyle of an American backpacker and decided to live as cheaply and as adventurous as possible over the next two and a half months. Reed agreed with me as we sat on the bleacher-like seating of the food truck emporium along the

Copenhagen canal and watched the intricate sunset of that early autumn night.

    Earlier in the day we switched our hostel from the party hostel to one built in the 1700s, it used to be a brothel in the Nyhavn district but was then turned into something of a nicer hostel. Through the dimming light of late September Reed and I spoke about what we had seen that day and reminisced on similarities between the rest of Scandinavia. The new hostel, the old brothel, was luxury compared to the party hostel. Quiet and accommodating, the new hostel's dormitory had the same amount of bunkbeds but with the simple addition of curtains on the beds to add that extra layer of privacy.

    Somehow the two of us got the last bunk in the room full of sleeping, scratching men and I ducked into my curtained bottom bunk and Reed slowly crawled into he bunk atop of mine. Settling in for a quiet nights rest I pull out my phone and look up news in the contiguous countries of Europe. Refugees were crossing the borders of Hungary, Greece, Sweden, and numerous others across the continent. Some countries were predicting shutdowns of their borders while others were promising free passage. I found my eyes growing heavy as they scanned the alternating views dancing across the bright screen with the dark faces and the children looking directly into the camera with fear and panic. It would only be a few months until I faced the crisis myself.

    The next day, the final day of Reed and I as a pair, I woke to a relatively quiet room. Like so many days before, I stumbled out of the room away from the comfort and warmth of my bed and into the lobby to find Reed sitting in an overstuffed chair drinking a coffee with an intelligent stare gazing off into nothing. Our eyes meet for the last morning and we smiled as we greeted the day for one last time in Europe. We both knew that day was the final one, so what to do?

Leaving the hostel which used to be a brothel in the Nyhavn district of Copenhagen, we strolled lazily past the pedestrians in the early morning sunshine and were happy, if not satisfied, by all that had happened in the past two weeks. Slowly, we walked towards the downtown area and eventually end up near the Central Station, the departure point for both of us the following day at different times. It happened to be free admission day at the National Museum and we decided to take advantage and took hours admiring the dense collection of Danish history ranging from pottery, which so happens to be on the currency in our pockets, to swords, to modern day advances. I found the museum fascinating which spurred thoughts of how young our own country is, at least those people who I descend from, and keep gazing at millennia presented before us.

Once through the National Museum we trekked the distance to the Carlsberg Brewery grounds, one of the largest breweries in Europe and the intricate museum in which the grounds are held. We paid the obscene ticket prices, every purchase over ten euros sends the disappointed face of the Australian wayfarer to mind. Reed and I spent hours gently pacing through the in-depth history of the Carlsberg Brewery ranging from technological advances to the history of their bottles. We saw where their prize-winning horses are kept as well as the backstory of their beautiful architecture. For a couple of beer nerds the tour was a success and taught us much in the way of traditional brewing techniques and even came with two beer tickets included.

The golden skies turned to overcast gray clouds as we left the brewery.. Having already booked a second night at the Nyhavn hostel we were secured a room and were lackadaisical with our responsibilities. Near the brewery we found a market and ate. We left talking about the future and how everything which had happened over the last fourteen days seemed to be a blur of images dazzling across a wormhole from the distant hop fields of Oregon to the pastel painted buildings of Nyhavn.

As had happened numerous times over the course of the summer, my head went a buzz with the effects of alcohol and the air smelled crisp and full of opportunity and everlasting ambition. But what were the two of us to do on our last night in Europe as a pair of intrepid travelers forging our way through the footpaths of a distant land? The answer was simple as Reed led us to one of the pristine brewing establishments in the north of Europe.

The bar was lined with a shining hardwood floor stretching out leading to matte black finished steel beams and Edison-bulbed light fixtures dangling elegantly over well-dressed, well-groomed patrons with frothy drinks before them, smiles exciting their faces and looks of gluttonous joy in their eyes. We walked toward the beautiful barkeep, her eyes flirting by darting downward then up again over cheek crinkles and beneath curled brunette hair. The three of us signed the social contract by saying our salutations and were soon sipping curiously from the taster tray of six beers brought for our enjoyment.

Over the course of two hours we sat at the bar drinking our beers slowly and deliberately, commenting on each one. A strange mix of emotions flooded over me and I was caught off guard. On the one hand was a welling isolation, one that had not quite reached fruition but something lurking out in the distance which I knew would overtake me once the sun rose the following day. The other hand held a feeling I was not expecting, confident joy. It wasn't a joy that's weight was felt by Reed leaving but, instead, a joy felt by the act of forging alone into an unknown so outside my comfort zone it was borderline unbearable to think too much about before anxiety welled and made me sweat.

Up until then my life had been one of a yearning for those out-of-my-zone experiences, fishing in Alaska or farming in the foothills of eastern Oregon, but this feeling was different; it was immense in a real way, one measured by miles instead of by emotion. What lay ahead of me through the rest of Europe wasn't merely a series of trains, planes, and automobiles but a vast network of me winding through the chaos of several countries with their own traditions and languages and people all to forge an experience I would keep with me until the day I died.

Sitting on that barstool I looked back at what Reed and I had already done and was immensely proud at the amount we had stuffed into such a short amount of time. In only a few hours he would leave my side and I would break off into that ether of the unknown and drift on without any form of a lifeline. There was a power in that and also a fear, a dread which told me I could fail and have to call my trip early, leaving the continent with my tail between my legs and a failure to follow. As I looked off into the distant void slowly sipping from a taster glass Reed must have sensed my worry and began rattling off how excited he was for what was to come for me and the stories I would tell once we reunited back in Oregon, back home.

I smiled wide and took him up on the offer of forgetting my worry and we went back to drinking the beers and enjoying our last night of European drinking. We left that bar with my head light and bladder full. The walk back toward the brothel-turned-hostel was cool and the moon peeked through the clouds casting its shimmering glow off the canal of Nyhavn. Our hostel was quiet and the front desk held a young man half asleep reading a book giving us a nod as we walked on toward our dorm. The room was filled with quiet snores and the two of us stood beside our curtained bunk awkwardly for a few seconds before blurting out something about "I'll be seeing you back home" and "hope everything goes well." Awkward smiles and giggles replaced the requisite hug and pats on the back.

I crawled into my bunk and closed the curtain. Sleep came suddenly from the drink and without realizing it the dark had given way to a light which spread ferociously from the window overlooking the boats along the canal. I quickly found my phone and saw it was eight o'clock, Reed had been gone for almost four hours and I was alone in Europe.

A strand of long, greasy hair fell into my eyes and I ran a sweaty hand through it to push it back with the rest of my curled, dank locks. As had happened the night before, the first feeling which came over me was one of dread but I didn't like it, I pushed it back and forced myself to take in the beauty which lay before me. A wanderlust had been brewing in the depths of me for so long and here I stood at a precipice looking up at a grand adventure, one which could truly tame that vagabond lifestyle I had yearned for.

 I smiled and ducked my head, more greasy curls fell over my eyes and I left them there. The person I had always dreamed of becoming was sitting in a hostel far from home and the only thing holding him back was a flimsy curtain.

 I walked out of that hostel with headphones in and a swagger in every footloose step. I was alone in Europe and I couldn't wait to experience every adventure which lay before me.

PART II

ALONE

Chapter 8

Germany

The sun shone bright upon my face as I left the hostel with music blasting in my headphones bolstering the confidence welling up deep within my core. It was relatively early in the morning, especially by tourist standards, and the sidewalks were free of the bustle and hurry which I had come to recognize as the Nyhavn district. Instead, many shopkeepers were sweeping their stoops or adjusting their sandwich boards in the ways that seemed to have worked for them in the past. The water in the canal winked an intense glimmer as I walked over a bridge and along my way into the downtown area of Copenhagen, past the city hall surrounded by corporate billboards and American fast food and coffee establishments, into the rush of people and traffic, and finally into the traveling circus that was the central station.

So many people, so many different nationalities and languages collided into a cacophony of sound distracting enough for even the most seasoned traveler to be nudged off kilter. With the confidence of a weary adventurer I stepped forth into the chaos knowing full well I could conquer, after all I had traveled throughout Scandinavia and lived to tell about it, why couldn't I do the same on my solo expedition through the heart of Europe?

It was that confidence which was masking my sadness and overwhelming feeling of isolation at not having Reed by my side. The mask was paper thin but I didn't know it until after my third round around the station without seeing my bus listed in all the usual places. With a reassuring breath I calmed myself down and worked up the courage to speak to one of the workers of the central station to ask for assistance.

As nice as possible I asked the Danish woman, uniform tucked neatly and hat pulled down tight, where I might find my bus. A rickety smile wavered on my face as she impolitely told me the bus I was looking for was a third-party outfit and they didn't have anything to do with them so I would have to find it on my own. Once she finished, she promptly walked away to attend to one of the other poor souls which should be so unfortunate as to meet that woman in their time of need.

With a panic I looked at my phone and saw I only had ten minutes until departure. SHIT! I thought to myself as I tried to gather my bearings and not freak out. With a procession of deep breaths I started to retrace my steps from when I purchased the ticket only a couple of hours before. As the minutes ticked by, my fingers raced across my phone's screen until I found a map with the departure location marked by a green circle. According to the map the bus was very close so I hitched my small pack and ran out of the large doors of the station onto the bustling sidewalks filled with smiling families and angsty backpackers huddled en masse. Like a running back breaking through the line I split through the by standers glancing quickly at my phone, gauged the direction which to follow and set off for the bus with beads of sweat mounting beneath my hairline.

It was now only three minutes until departure and the bus was nowhere in sight. I had already made one revolution around the station, crossed over the main tracks, descended a grimy staircase, and tried reading signs and symbols with little help. Finally, from a 100 yards away, I saw the green bus parked beneath a street sign which matched my ticket with the words "HAMBURG" running along the front window. Sudden shock came over my body and I began walking…then jogging…then full on sprinting toward my transport to a new land. With the bus getting closer my nerves began to dissipate and joy spread throughout my head, I was going to make it.

As I got to the opposite side of the street, the bus idling across, I saw the driver buckle his seat belt and begin pulling the bus away from the curb. With a jolt I yelled in my most confident voice "STOP….PLEASE STOP" but all I received in return was the driver looking me in the eyes with the most apathetic of stares and with a shrug of his shoulders he turned the wheel guiding the bus slowly away.

Like a character from a romantic comedy I began sprinting as fast as I could along after the bus. With my heart pounding and my thighs clenching I chased the bus down about a block before he turned a corner and was out of my sight. I stood in the center of the road with tears in my eyes and my headphones dangling onto the dirty asphalt. It was my first true solo experience in Europe and I had completely failed.

Looking around, defeated, I pulled my headphones from the street and plodded toward the sidewalk. I stood there wanting to cry, wanting to give up and go home and call it a vacation. There had already been so much I had seen, why couldn't I just call up my mom and ask her for money to bring me back to safety? Just then an overwhelming desire surged deep within me, the same feeling which came to me when I was in twenty foot seas in Alaska or underneath a tractor in the August heat of eastern Oregon. It was a surge which put into perspective everything which was going on around me and how important a situation, or better yet how important my reaction to a certain situation, was at a particular time and place. This feeling told me I wasn't just a person on vacation who screwed up and who could go home but instead, I was an adventurer, a backpacker on a pilgrimage to find out more about myself than to see pretty sights.

I wiped the tears from my eyes and breathed deep while walking back to the central station. Like Reed had taught me before, I found the purchasing booth, bought a train ticket to Hamburg for three times more than my bus ticket had been (I vowed to never let that happen again) and I waited patiently for the two hours to pass until I boarded the train.

As the train left Copenhagen I smiled wide, not from adventure but from pride. Not only had I failed my first solo duty in Europe by missing my bus but I also had overcome the first obstacle of my solo journey. It is never the destinations which makes the adventure but the journey along the way and the fuck-ups one endures and overcomes which makes the ride a whole lot sweeter.

Traveling through rural Denmark my train soon found itself boarding a ferry which would take us across a wide channel into Germany. After the train boarded the ship, which was a strange feeling hard to wrap my mind around, all the passengers exited the train and scattered throughout the ferry. I climbed to the top deck and watched as the ship left the shore of one country, sailed across the channel with the blue sky above and the crystal sun glistening off the water below, and within no time reached the shores of Germany. Like before, all the passengers boarded the train and we railed through country side, which gave way to suburbs, and finally to the bustling city of Hamburg.

As Reed was the navigator in our duo, I hadn't thought to look into the location of my hostel or, for that matter, the location of anything in the city which I vastly underestimated in size. Instead, when I departed the train I was met with an overwhelming rush of people speaking a rough sounding language and a phone map which would not register. I stood along a wall right outside the train station watching as people spewed in and out of the doors looking up at signs with impossible to read names and no idea where to begin walking toward my hostel which I was due in less than an hour.

Gathering myself I finally found a tourist shop and grabbed the free sightseeing map and used my hostel receipt to pinpoint its actual location. Off I went, trying my best to harness the energy which comes from new experiences, through the clean streets of Hamburg, up hills, through city parks, and into a graffiti strewn neighborhood. Between a painting of an anarchist symbol and some kind of punk art featuring a rusty bicycle and a musical instrument far removed from playing quality sat nestled a dingy hostel I would be calling home for the night.

With mild trepidation I ventured into the near decrepit building's office and was met by a balding, scrawny man with a rough looking face. I showed him my passport then he began berating me for being late (which was fair, it was about two hours past when I said I would show up) and how lucky I was to not have my room given up in the meantime. In my head I thought how ridiculous that statement was, judging by the disarray of the outside plus the insides mess I couldn't see people clamoring to stay at his luxury resort of a hostel.

Once the formalities were finalized he escorted me up the rickety elevator which needed a key to operate and along the dormitory halls leaving me at the door with the first smile I had seen from the man since arriving. I walked into the large room to find four single beds spaced far apart. Two of the beds had people on them, one was a handsome young guy from Turkey and the other was a mousy Romanian of similar age. We exchanged pleasantries and I dropped my pack on a vacant bed. It wasn't long before we were all talking about ourselves.

It turned out both young men were going to the same college and both were studying political science. Due to the number of incoming students there was a housing shortage on the campus so many found themselves living in hostels, such as our grand establishment, paying much more than they would at the school until a room opened up or a roommate could be found off campus. The two seemed okay with the situation and talk quickly turned to the nature of how I had come to Hamburg.

I told them all about my travels thus far and my ambitions to see a vast amount of Europe in the upcoming months. They seemed vaguely interested but their eyes really sparked when the Romanian asked about American politics, "is your country really serious about Donald Trump?"

It was the fall of 2015 and in a year's time America would elect its next president so I had been preparing for this and other similar questions leading up to the Europe trip.

The three of us debated politics, those of America and the rest of Europe, and I was impressed by how much both of the young men knew about my country and how little, to an embarrassing degree, I knew of theirs.

Time flew by and before long sun was beginning to set and the Turkish guy got dressed in nice clothes explaining his use of a phone app which got him dates with young ladies who would be down to hook up with no strings attached. I was impressed by the luck he had had in the past and the stories of his exploits were graphic and numerous. As he left I gathered some essentials and left the mousy

Romanian to his political books while I hit the streets of Hamburg.

The first stop was food. Reed had been talking about currywurst and how great it was in Germany from even before our departure to Europe. I wandered through the punk streets of my neighborhood until I found a small restaurant. Not knowing what they served I decided to give it a chance. It paid off and within minutes I was sitting next to a window with a boat full of salted french fries, fantastic sausage, and a heaping pile of sweet curry. The meal was cheap, filling, and utterly delicious all perfect for a backpacker.

Due to the astronomically high price of alcohol in northern Europe I had to be semi-sparing with our consumption of the grand elixirs. But, now in continental Euope, alcohol was back to being cheap and easy to find. Understanding this I found a grocery store, bought a cheap bottle of red wine and headed back to my hostel. Along the way the bars and restaurants were spilling over into the streets and young people with pink mohawks and combat boots stumbled together with beer cans in hand walking past their comrades which had already consumed too much drink and were sprawled sickly in the gutters. Music filled the air and the smell of sausage mixed with urine and vomit; it all seemed to feel right.

I spent the rest of the night in the garden of the hostel drinking red wine, listening to the mixing of music from the neighborhood, and writing in my journal. The words flowed from the pen with ease, so much had already happened and being alone wasn't as bad as I had thought.

Morning came with a jarring awakening as I looked at my phone and sighed at how early it was. I looked around the room and saw a mass where the Romanian was, an empty bed where the lucky Turk had been, and the third bed, which had been empty the night before, now housed an old man with a large belly and nothing on but his raggedy boxer shorts, snoring. It took me a few seconds to gather myself, it had not ceased to be strange to awaken in a room with people who had not been there before, it was absolutely the worst part of hostel life. I quietly got ready and gladly traded the snoring man for a crisp morning in the sun.

The streets smelled even more of piss and vomit than the evening before but the bakeries were producing smells of home and comfort which I couldn't deny. I walked into one and watched as a mother and her young daughter picked out their treat for the day. It was nice to experience someone else's normal life in a foreign land and made me yearn for the normalcy which I hoped would ensue once I made it back home.

The warm woman behind the counter smiled and through numerous hand gestures I left with a cinnamon roll and black coffee. I walked happily along the sidewalks not having a clue of where I was going. There was a man with an eye patch playing an accordion under a bridge and I thought how cinematic life is sometimes. Before long I came to an urban park underneath a tall white spire and watched as frogs jumped along lily pads and rabbits scurried between bushes.

Nearing the main area of town, the place I had first ventured from the train station, I heard numerous church bells tolling and turned toward the sounds. I passed a large water feature with sail boats dreamily floating from one end to the other while parents played with their children along the edges and young people held beers and leaned on one another soaking up their youth and the moment of *now*.

Further I walked and found a neighborhood of canals and brick buildings along their edges. Large ships, transformed from their time at sea into restaurants and bars, beckoned passersby to come aboard for a drink. A bridge with so many locks along its wire railings professed little notes of love and hearts and ambitions and like a sign from the love gods a young couple passed along holding hands and the girl gently placed her head against his shoulder and I couldn't help but think of home and all that could have been and how if it had been then I wouldn't be there then. Retrospect is strange.

Canals gave way to busy business streets and tall buildings and people in suits as my walking kept taking me to places vastly different. I had heard drinking in public was legal in Germany so I bought a can of German pilsner and strutted along drinking deep from the shining can and feeling odd but free. Soon I stumbled onto a street devoted to the sex trade and couldn't help but follow a group of white haired men and women along its path. In every window the letters "XXX" were a glow in neon and pornographic words and pictures adorned sandwich boards and marquees. I had no desire to partake in any of the shop's offerings but it felt nice to see such things being advertised in blatant ways and made me wish my own country wasn't so afraid of such natural urges and desires.

The day was coming to an end and I paid a visit to the currywurst shop near my hostel. With a six-pack of cheap beer I took the rickety elevator up and entered my room expecting company but was relieved to find none. Remembering what the front desk man had told me about their laundry service, I gathered the few clothes I had and took them down to a corner of the lobby, went back and took a shower. A couple of hours later a knock at my door brought my clothes back clean and I spent the rest of the night quietly alone with cold beer and a documentary on Ernest Hemingway. It was my first night truly alone in almost three weeks.

With clean clothes and the shower from the night before I felt like a human as I hurried along the morning streets, past the one eyed accordion player, through the streets lined with churches, and made it to the *proper* bus station with time to spare. Never wanting to experience a debacle like the one had in Copenhagen, I vowed to better plan for the transportation segments of my journey but not at the expense of the spontaneity of every other part.

The bus left Hamburg and sped along the autobahn on our way to Berlin. We arrived a short time later and were dropped off in a residential neighborhood which I had not expected. Once again I had made a mess of my planning and after a few frantic moments of feeling completely lost I gathered my bearings and saw I was five miles from my hostel.

Pissed at myself I trudged on through the morning heat, going through neighborhoods not on any travel agencies "Must See" lists. After what felt like a lifetime I saw a group of people huddled around an old wall without signs or fanfare declaring what the big deal was. Curious, I turned into the area and soon found information plaques and dug out areas showing excavated rooms and tunnels and was surprised to be standing at a section of the Berlin Wall. I spent an hour reading all of the information boards and staring at the sick beauty of the demolished divider which fell the year I was born.

My hostel was nearby and before long I was at the front desk behind two party girls in their early twenties listening to them talk about which club they would "hit up" in a few hours. The girls left cackling and shaking their asses in their skin tight jeans and I bellied up to the desk with my week old scraggly beard, red loose fitting beanie, and bags under my eyes asking for a room. With a smile the young woman sent me down the hall with a key and I opened the door to a tight space filled with four bunk beds, six beds already taken. I threw my bag on the top bunk next to the window and I introduced myself to the friendly young people already in the room.

Directly across from me was a cute German girl with red bobbed hair and freckles under her eyes. She was the first to introduce herself and ask where I was from. Underneath her was an English girl dressed in all black with books spilling out of her backpack. On the same wall as my bunk was an Indian guy with a thick accent and a wonderful demeanor, obviously sharp and well-educated. The bunk above him was vacant and across from that was a quiet Australian girl who didn't say much and was buried in a book. Below her sat the oldest person in the room, maybe forty and Australian, a man who thought quite a lot of himself and was only in Berlin to party.

The seven of us talked for an hour about our travels, how the English girl was studying abroad, the Indian was taking a holiday before university, the German girl was studying at a local university and couldn't find boarding, and how I was country hopping to find out more about myself but in the end was running away from the later years of my twenties and the responsibilities held within.

After the hour of non-stop talking finished the Australian man sprayed half a bottle of cologne on his too-tight shirt and gave one more look in the mirror before leaving for the night. Silence followed and I quickly unloaded my belongings onto my bunk and departed out into the waning sunlight, determined to see the sights.

The first stop had to be the Brandenberg Gate which was quite close and why I spent the few dollars extra on my hostel. With time to spare I made it to the gate and was met by hundreds of tourists trying to capture the remarkable photo I was, the gate at sunset. Once satisfied, I weaved my way through the throng of people and hurried down to see the Victory Column. The long stretch of road began to darken as fellow tourists with cameras in hand began running to snap a final photo of the day. I reached the busy intersection just in time to catch the purple clouds mix with the orange of the dropping sun.

    Without a celestial deadline I explored the Column up close, saw the bullet holes still chipped into its sides, and left feeling the gravity of the city I was in and the scattered history of a time not so long ago. I made my way back to the Brandenburg Gate, which now had far less people, and stood admiring the craftsmanship and beauty of the architecture. The streets of Berlin were so clean and mixed with the crisp night air and close to cloudless sky the aura felt welcoming and pristine. Before heading back to my hostel I stood long looking at the Berlin Cathedral and how much like a castle it resembled.

    I made it back to my room with the lights on and conversation flowing. There was a vending machine in the lobby which sold cheap German beer and I came back with a few cans cold and sweating in my arms. The night went on for some time talking about European politics, French hipsters, and how there is no such thing as free water in Germany. The lights went out well after midnight as my head was swirling and the conversation of the day replayed over and over in my mind. I thought of the young girls I had seen earlier and wondered where they ended up and if their clubs and expensive drinks gave them as much joy as my cheap living, dirty backpacking lifestyle was giving me.

The light from the curtained window shone right into my eyes as I looked at my phone and saw the demonic numbers "7:30" display black against a white background. I, and I imagine the rest of the room, were jolted awake by the party-hard Australian slamming our door, pulling off his shoes, literally throwing himself into his bunk then proceeding to snore extremely loud. Beds creaked as bodies rolled over angrily, I tried the same tactic but knew instantly it wasn't worth it, I was awake and the day's countdown had begun. I slipped off the top bunk and instantly felt my brain clang back and forth against my dehydrated skull, another morning another hangover. I readied myself and was out into the German sunshine without hesitation, passed a beagle in a wheelchair, and continued on to the nearest bakery for black coffee and a pastry.

With my head remedied by the early morning chill, I rushed down to the Brandenburg Gate, the Victory Column, Charlottesburg Palace, and by noon was in a large park with a farmer's market going on. In dire need of clothes, I walked up and down the aisles of tents and awnings taking in the exotic smells of food and goods, most of which I had never seen. After a couple of trips through, I purchased socks from an old Gypsy woman with sparkling eyes and an easy smile who wished me luck with the rest of my travels.

Still in need of shirts I ventured into a nearby mall and purchased two shirts, each depicting different scenes of Americana, one Portland, Oregon and the other a series of photos of the California Redwoods. I explained to the apathetic German teen behind the counter how cool it was to buy shirts depicting my home so far away but all I got was a couldn't-care-less smirk and an outstretched hand wanting money.

The rest of the day was spent wandering through various residential areas of metropolitan Berlin, trying to watch a movie at a gigantic IMAX megaplex, settling on donuts instead, and heading back to my hostel to read and plan the next leg of my trip. It turns out not every day of a three month adventure has to be crazy, as long as the day ends with a greater appreciation for life and a growth of human spirit it is a success.

Almost exactly as the morning previous, my last day in Berlin began at seven with the partying Australian coming back to the hostel and snoring loudly. Without the hangover I saw the opportunity and made it out the door faster than the day previous feeling like I had gotten a great start on winning the morning.

The first part of the day was spent chasing cathedrals, their chiming bells guiding me along the way. Once I had my fill, I went to Museum Island and refused to pay the ridiculous price of admission so I walked around looking at the ornate architecture and statues all over the grounds. On one of my wanderings from the island to a restaurant I walked along a canal, through a couple of tunnels, and came across an old black man beautifully playing his trumpet at the far end of the final tunnel made bright by so much graffiti. I stopped and semi-hid myself against a wall of his tunnel and listened to the music swell and recede with joy then tragedy. That is the thing about large cities, no matter where you end up there is something to catch your eye, something amazing and something which will stand out far beyond the sights or what lie in a museum.

In the early afternoon I made it back to the IMAX theatre where the line was much more manageable and decided to go ahead and watch the American movie which would soothe my homesickness. I emerged from the cinema feeling glad in where I was and the decision I made to travel to Europe but sad in hearing the familiar American accents while I walked amongst the myriad others every day.

Like a sign from the heavens a McDonald's reared its ugly, golden arched-head at the most inopportune time and the feelings of home and comfort swelled. I sat and devoured a Big Mac and thought of home and the daily lives all those I knew were leading. I left the dingy establishment feeling a bit more whole and made my way toward the bus depot which would take me to Poland.

With time to spare I ventured through a large park with beautiful statues of famous people from Germany's past. It felt nice to walk through nature and enjoy the time of calm before the chaos inherent in country hopping. I emerged from the park near the the Victory Column and watched as the lady on top danced against the sunset of my last few hours in Berlin. Darkness fell over the city as I walked through increasingly sketchy neighborhoods until I arrived at the main bus depot.

The people milling about the depot could have been extras from a slick British gangster film with their shifty eyes and curious demeanors. These were people who were traveling on the cheap and I imagine some were either running from something or someone in their lives who may not have had the best intentions. After an hour of waiting my bus showed up, a double decker rig with two drivers who smelled of stale cigarettes and cheap coffee. I boarded and found my seat on the second story of the bus. We pulled out of the station along the twinkling street lamps of Berlin.

    I watched as the bright lights of the city began to diminish until there was only the darkness of the country landscape and a cloud blocked moon to guide us.

Chapter 9

Poland

The bus had been rocking back and forth on its trek from Germany to Poland for hours now and I hadn't slept. It has always been hard for me to sleep on a moving vehicle, especially on an adventure. There is always too much to see, too much to take in. In the five and a half hour ride I had probably logged three hours and when we pulled into Gdansk at 5:47 am I was feeling less than my best. The bus stopped outside the main train station, Gdansk Glowny, and the motley crew of bus travelers funneled off. Most riders had cars waiting for them or a home to go to but I had not planned on getting to the town so early and I had nowhere to go.

    A minor panic came over me. It was still dark, extremely cold and once again my phone's map wouldn't load after working fine back in Berlin. Regaining my wits I walked into the train station and found a McDonald's. I knew they would have Wi-Fi and something warm to eat so I ordered my meal, found a spot, plugged my phone in and began to plan the day. Once I was settled I looked around at the people frequenting a fast food chain that early in the morning. Most of the people looked like any business person or traveler you would see anywhere but then my eye caught a young woman in the booth behind me completely passed out. Super skinny with shaggy brown hair clumped and falling onto her face with arm extended out across the table she seemed to be completely out of her mind on some drug, probably heroin. Not long after a manager came over and tried waking her to no avail. The man came back with a female colleague and they picked the girl up and out the door they went.

    After the warm coffee began to work its magic and I had saved screenshots of the tourist spots of Gdansk and my hostel's location it was around seven and I decided to explore. The great part about traveling for so long and not having any plans is the freedom from time. It was a Thursday in the early morning which meant the city was populated not by nosy tourists but by everyday Polish people doing their thing and getting ready for the day. Walking from the train station into the downtown district I walked amongst business people in nice clothes and into the tourist area with shop keepers cleaning their windows getting ready for the day.

    The architecture in the downtown district was beautifully old and unique. They buildings were skinny with a façade topping which slanted up with sharp angles like something from Edward Gorey or Tim Burton. The ambiance of the district felt gothic and bleak but in a way which had charm and warmth. The cobblestones met my feet with a roughness which complemented the stark yet vibrant colors on the buildings above me. Totally lost in the beauty I walked underneath a large arch and found myself along a large canal stretching to the Gulf of Danzig. Along this canal was a strange building made of wood which was massive and had an overhang reaching above the large canal.

Fascinated, I walked towards the behemoth and soon found it to be a crane, more specifically a medieval port crane. I was mesmerized by the shape and size plus the buildings around it and the way the entire canal looked in the early morning light. With plenty of time to spare until I could check into my hostel I walked all over the old town district, a pretty simple feat since it is quite small, then headed over into the more residential region of Gdansk.

Like so often in tourist cities the downtown areas are filled with shops and bars and people with smiles on their faces but once you get out of these areas the residential spots are where the city shows its true face. Not long after I escaped the beauty of the old town I found myself in a poverty stricken place with run down, Cold War era apartments which looked grim and depressing. The people on that side of the canal lacked the smiles and brightness their fellow downtown compatriots had back with the crane and brick-strewn arches. There the markets had bars on their windows and the buildings were painted gray. Grim, it seemed like nothing had changed for a very long time.

Having seen enough of the residential area I turned a corner and began to head back toward the canal. Walking past what seemed to be a small industrial area I happened to see two men exchange money for a small package. Their eyes snapped to me, they said something discreetly to themselves, and the man who was handed the small package began walking quickly toward me. Panic came over me and I hurried back to the old town, the safe innards of the city where things were brighter and still shined. On the way, I looked over my shoulder and saw the man behind me but after turning down this street and that he was gone. Once amongst the camera toting tourists of the downtown I finally felt safe.

    I found a small diner in the middle of an open area in the old town district, ordered a large beer, food, and sat charging my phone in a booth looking out into the courtyard just in case the man with the package decided to cross my path again. After an hour the beers dulled my anxieties and I embarked on the long trek to my hostel.

    The hostel turned out to be farther than I had expected and after about three miles trek on a foot path running alongside a pair of train tracks I saw the sign for the hostel. Walking in I was greeted by an extremely nice lady who insisted on being called 'Mama.' I checked in and was given a tour. The first floor was where Mama and Papa lived and essentially ran the hostel. Ascending the staircase we made our way to the second floor where the bedrooms and showers were located, some bunk beds others single rooms. The third floor was the living room with an impressive rack of movies, a large TV, the kitchen and crates of vinyl records. Mama left me with a key and I walked into my room.

Four people around my age stood looking at a map with three bunk beds lining the walls around them. We all exchanged pleasantries and I threw my backpack on the top bunk and we soon dove into conversation. After a while 'Papa' came up and introduced himself and we talked about his love for the Grateful Dead and I brought up my old fishing boat captain from Alaska being a Dead Head and we instantly became friendly. An awkward man with a bald head and a ragged ponytail jetting down his back he always wore a tie dye shirt and exuded an aura of warmth shared equally by Mama, his wife. After Papa, the name he insisted we all call him, talked to everyone in the room he asked me to go to the backyard with him so he could show me a Dead Head flag he took to all of the concerts he had attended.

Once in the large, well-manicured backyard he asked if I smoked marijuana and I told him no and he looked confused. Here I was a backpacking American with a beanie and shoulder length curly hair coming out the back who liked the Dead but didn't smoke weed. Shrugging, Papa said "okay" in his muffled accented way and showed me his Dead Head flag and talked about the concerts he had seen and his love for Jerry Garcia. It was getting late and I decided to find some food and curl up in bed as multi-colored bears danced through my mind as a melodic guitar played the Dead in my head.

The next day I devoted to myself. No walking around aimlessly, no photos, no adventures. Just me sitting on my tablet working on getting caught up on my fledgling blog and sorting through photos of the past few countries. I took all my gear to the third floor and, being Friday, no one was there. I spread out and started sorting through Papa's CD collection. It was as if the entire music scene of the sixties were confined to those few crates with everything from the Grateful Dead, Jimi Hendrix, Janis Joplin, Cream and The Doors. I pulled out the first Doors album then found the second then the third and before I knew it all six studio albums with Jim Morrison at the helm were laid out in front of me. For years "The Doors" had been the answer to the ever-present "Whose your favorite band?" question and to be in a hippie hostel with a couple of days relaxation and writing to get caught up on I couldn't believe my luck.

As soon as the first album began funneling through the speakers I began to sort through photos from the previous countries and write about what had been happening. As the photos began floating in the files Jim Morrison's vocals filled the room with their haunting, shamanic sound. I played each album in its entirety and sorted through thousands of photos. Papa came up once to see who had unleashed The Doors upon his hostel and we talked about how amazing they were and the impact they had upon the world. Through his John Lennon glasses and a small smirk he said his usual, monotoned "okay" and disappeared.

In the evening people came lazily through the living room area and I decided to stop playing the music over the speakers and concentrate on writing. Eventually my roommate from Columbia sat on the couch beside me with a girl I had not yet seen and they began making conversation.

The girl had just flown in from London and was going to be staying in Gdansk for a few days since she and the Columbian guy were old friends. They had met some time ago on an island off of Honduras while they were both getting their SCUBA diving instructor licenses. The English girl was flamboyant and loud with equally boisterous red-hair accentuated by a thick accent. It was obvious she was a partier and loved to have a good time. The three of us talked until late that night and I agreed to stay an extra day in northern Poland on account of my do-nothing day.

Early the next morning I booked my train to Krakow and hostel there for the next day. As I was going through the mundanity of scheduling the couple from the night before came up and invited me to go with them to Malbork, a town not far from Gdansk with a massive castle from the 13th century. We asked Mama and Papa the easiest way of getting there and they told us there was a train close to the hostel and gave us a time sheet. We packed our things and made our way to the tracks with what we thought was plenty of time to spare. We were wrong.

With the tracks in sight we saw our train come and go. We had misread the schedule and had another few hours until the next train to Malbork would arrive. Without missing a beat the English girl suggested we get beers and head back to the hostel to wait. Arriving back to the hostel we sat in the backyard in the early October sun and talked about traveling and where we would all go for our next adventures. The two made the SCUBA island sound appealing and we talked about their time on the island most of the train ride to Malbork. The last half of the trip they both slept and made me the lookout for the right stop.

 The town of Malbork is fairly small and felt a bit like the residential area of Gdansk. Not having really planned the trip we weren't sure where the castle was located but soon asked some people and were on our way. As we came closer we saw numerous military grade trucks pass by and it felt like we shouldn't have been where we were. Not long after the trucks passed we found the beautiful, red-tinted castle and made our way down toward the draw bridge. We were too late to get the audio tour so we had to go into the castle blind and with none of us doing any research on the castle it was more about admiring the beauty than the actual history of the grand building.

 In Scandinavia Reed and I had gone to a few forts and before that I had only gone to forts in America so the Malbork castle, for me, was thrilling. The same can be said for our Columbian companion as it was his first true castle as well but the girl from England was not nearly as impressed at the fact it *was* a castle but how grand the grounds really were. Walking through the front draw bridge we came upon the massive courtyard and brick which stretched on for days. The intricacies of the sculptures and the gardens were astonishing along with the detail of the floor tiles with their intricate designs sprawling and matching the rising columns who too had defined designs all along their height. We spent a couple of hours walking through the gigantic building traversing its numerous staircases and large cavernous rooms. As we left I smiled and was glad to have gone on my first stranger-to-friend adventure.

The three of us grabbed some food then headed back to our train and back to Gdansk. Discussions of traveling came up again and we discussed where our next stops would be. Mine would be a train down to Krakow in the southern regions of Poland. The English girl would head back to work in London and our Columbian companion would stay in Poland for a bit longer then move to Barcelona and stay in Spain for school.

Mama and Papa both greeted us when we returned to the hostel, their cheery eyes and smiles made us happy and content. I went to the third floor and made sure my reservations for the trip south were in order and began writing once again. The night set in and as soon as I closed my tablet a young couple from England walked through the third floor door.

The couple turned out to be a guy and a girl, both 18 years old, from England traveling for their gap year. They too had come to Gdansk from Berlin on the same overnight bus I had taken but their experience in Berlin had been much different. Being so young their main purpose in travel was to have the best time possible at whatever the cost. If that meant taking speed then heading to an exclusive punk rock party in the innards of Berlin then that is what they did. My form of traveling was different. Up until that point I had not gone to a club nor had I really partied. The goal of my travel was to see as many important sights and learn as much about the culture of each place I visited. No drugs, little money and great distances to travel.

We talked for a couple of hours and it made me appreciate the differences in our age. If I had done my same trip when I was their age as opposed to doing it when I was twenty-six, the trip would have been vastly different as well as much shorter plus I would have came home with a different standard for success.

The kids from England were great for what they were, kids. I was glad for the conversation and to hear their stories but also for the parallel they drew with their travels and mine. Maybe at eighteen my Grand European Adventure would have been different. Maybe I would have partied and spent money and embed in the drug scene. Maybe at twenty-six I was boring. More introverted. More grounded. But maybe, also, my maturity seeped into the cracks and made the adventure more robust and exuberant, more resistant to the lows and more excited for the highs. The more I talked to the youngsters from Britain the more I realized I was content with what I had done thus far and would do in the days and months to come.

I said goodbye to the partying two as they went out to find the next happening spot downtown while I packed all of my things to get ready for the early train ride the next morning. Maybe the things we learn as we get older make us boring but the experiences we have along the years will stay with us for a lifetime. As I laid in bed before sleep wrapped its warm fingers around my consciousness I couldn't help but smile at how far I had come and the adventures which lie ahead.

The hostel room had a smell of dank feet and was a bit musty from all the mouths opening and closing in their deep stages of sleep. I reached for my phone nestled under my pillow and saw it was only eight and I tried to roll over but two guys across the room were in a weird synchronized snoring pattern where as one breathed-in a rattling snore the other loudly exhaled something phlegm-laden.

Having gotten used to that kind of waking I rolled onto my back and began to write in my phone's journal what had happened the day before. My fingers flew, "11 hour train, started alone, then old granny and her grandson, then car was crammed with polish women, two backpackers in their 50's told me I was in their seat, they didn't like me, finally to Krakow tired and wore out...day 25."

Gathering a few essentials I quietly slid from the top bunk to the old wooden floor. Out the creaky door I found my way to the common room and opened my tablet to try to plan the day. It is always a weird feeling getting to a new town in the dark. Everything seems brand new and strange in a way which makes the night before seem like it didn't happen.

How had I found the hostel?
When did I check-in?
Who had I seen the night before?

After making a general plan of what sights to see and how to get to them I returned to the musty hostel room, grabbed my things and made my way out of the large wooden doors onto the streets of Krakow. Whereas Gdansk felt like walking around a museum with all of its preserved building fronts and old crane looming large Krakow felt like a working, living city bustling in the morning light trying to get things done. The hostel was located close to the old town district, Stare Miasto, so within a few minutes I was in the heart of the tourist sights. As was my mission along the trip I purposely didn't do research as to what to see so I could avoid being an absolute tourist.

As I walked amongst the people and the different colored buildings I kept feeling an air of something different. It didn't feel like a simple town and it didn't feel overly touristic. I kept walking and found myself surrounded by people my age with a look of intelligence and ambition in their eyes and soon found I was in the middle of the oldest university in Poland, Jagiellonian University. College campuses all over the world share that same feeling permeating the air. Everyone seems busy on these campuses and the ambiance feels like people have a purpose. I had not been on a college campus since Sweden and it felt good.

My mind began to buzz with ideas of future writing projects and photographs to take. With legs ever moving I passed all the young adults in their nice clothes and dapper European swag as I contrasted them with my "travel clothes" and felt dingy yet somehow proud of myself for living my own dream I had had for myself when I was on my own college campus. An almost Kerouacian ideal where a traveling intellectual could be in rough clothes and still pursue an art and a dream.

Soon those young people with bright eyes began to give way to older people with fanny packs and cameras hanging pendulous from their necks and I realized I was no longer on the campus proper but coming up to a large castle on a hilltop. Wawel Castle is a 14th century castle sitting large with red-tinted brick and high turrets. Similar in feeling to the Malbork Castle back in northern Poland it exuded an impressive air and I followed the gaggle of tourists up the hill towards its gate.

Before I came too close, I saw signs indicating payment for entrance and guides. Not wanting to spend the money on either, I went back down the hill and around to another entrance and walked through the gates. I didn't make it too far into the courtyard until my guilt took over and decided not to be a freeloader and returned down toward the river running through Krakow at the castles feet. Snapping a few photos I was hungry and decided to go back towards the university to find food.

After inhaling an entire pizza with a liter of beer I went in search of my next attraction. Crisscrossing all over the Stare Miasto and taking in the beautiful cathedrals and market squares and outside art I tired of the tourist scene and began taking random alleyways in search of something fresh. After a turn here and a turn there I found a bookstore. Throughout the trip I had been trying to find good books that weren't about traveling and were in English. It was surprisingly difficult and I had finished my last book in Germany. I walked in and was expecting to be greeted in

Polish but instead heard the beautiful, familiar sounds of English!

The bookstore was magnificent in every way. With the walls lined with bookshelves ten feet tall and a small café situated in the middle with books lying on sitting tables all around it the bookstore felt like something out of a dream. The man behind the counter of the café was a man from the UK with a smooth accent and crazy hair, the kind of person one would expect to see in such an establishment. A smile shot across my face as each book spine I read was in English and there were topics such as "The Beats" and "20th Century Writers" and "The Lost Generation."

Breaking my astonishment I walked to the café and ordered a latte and told the man how nice it was to stumble upon a bookstore such as his. We talked for a few moments while my drink was being made and I sat my backpack on the hardwood floor. I searched over the titles and finally found Hunter S Thompson's *Fear and Loathing on the Campaign Trail*. With book and latte in hand I made my way to the back of the surprisingly large store and found the reading room with people of all walks of life at small wooden tables with quaint reading lights on each.

The bookstore occupied two hours of my time while I sat relaxed, drinking my coffee and reading the book and taking in the people doing their own thing on their own time. Normalcy is so rare when traveling for a long period of time and whenever I found it I would take it in and relax as if a sudden bubble came over me blocking the outside world and warming me with its radiance. Stepping out from my meditative normalcy I said goodbye to the man behind the counter and made my way back to the hostel.

Walking through the lobby I asked if they had any openings for a tour of Auschwitz the following day, to which the girl behind the counter nodded and set up for me. Having my fill of traveling for the day I grabbed my tablet from my room and checked email. I had set up a reminder informing me when the 21 days was up from when I lost my bag back in Finland; that day was tomorrow. Having heard nothing from the airline since I filled out the initial missing luggage form I decided to write them an email just to cover my ass. Within an hour I received a response saying they had found my pack in the lost luggage section of the airport and because of that it had never been scanned which is why they hadn't informed me of it's disappearance!

In complete shock all I could respond with was a simple "thank you" and told them to send it to my mother's house back in Oregon since I couldn't say where I would be when they eventually got around to sending it. I sat back in my chair and thought back to the inconvenience not having that bag had caused but also how simple the fix would have been if I had emailed them sooner. The rest of the night was spent watching a documentary and thinking how many life lessons, some hard and some trivial, could be learned along this bout of traveling.

The next morning I awoke to the familiar sound of snoring. Loud, unstoppable snoring which only a hostel can produce. With the same routine as before, I quietly escaped the room over creaking floor boards, quickly readied as was out the large hostel door into the brisk morning haze. The shuttle to Auschwitz made its appearance as three girls, younger than myself and much more attractive, were making small talk on the sidewalk. We boarded the van, found our seats and sat in silence as anticipation stood thick amongst us.

The grizzled driver weaved through crowded streets picking up a thirty-something guy from one hostel and three seniors from another before embarking on towards Oświęcim, a small town about an hour's drive from Krakow which houses Auschwitz. As we left, the driver pulled down a screen from the roof of the shuttle and began playing a half hour video documenting the horrors of the holocaust and the history of the concentration camps. The atmosphere in the shuttle shifted from nice pleasantries in meeting new people to one of sadness and despair. We had all assumed this tour would be one of darkness and levity but none of us prepared for what we were to see.

The shuttle parked in a large lot and our tour guide, a mid-thirties Polish woman, came aboard directing us to merge with another group waiting nearby. All of our backpacks and purses were left in the shuttle and I had slung my camera around my neck like the rest of the tourists I had tried to avoid along the trip but in such cases where the importance of the experience would mean so much to myself and people back home the exception in my logic was made.

My group was probably twenty people strong and we moved toward the security line in one large mass with few words spoken between us. We were told to empty our pockets and go through a metal detector. The line kept shuffling along and soon we were given audio pieces to better hear our English speaking guide. Once the entire group was together again the tour guide in an understandably somber tone told us about the rules as to not touching the history surrounding us and to not take pictures in certain buildings and above all else to respect the lives lost on those grounds not so many years ago.

The wind was chilly as we came to the notorious entrance gate of the concentration camp with the phrase "Arbeit Macht Frei" (Work Makes You Free) donning the top of the iron gates in front of the sullen grey clouds in the sky. The barbed wire stretched black in every direction while attached to the metal posts looming high with a curved top pointing into the camp. The next hour was spent touring the blocks of Auschwitz with the halls covered in mugshots of prisoners, the mountains of eye glasses, boots, and poison canisters used to kill over a million people. We shuffled like curious specters through the infamous block 11 with its standing rooms and starvation cells all the while hearing our tour guide's grim voice go in and out of focus seemingly ricocheting off the walls and into our headphones so distant.

Walking along outside the cell blocks were hanging hooks where prisoner's wrists would be tied together, hung on the hooks with their bodies hanging unnaturally until their shoulder's would dislocate. Firing walls were still standing at the end of long alleys with flowers laid to honor the unknown number of humans shot dead at the wall's feet. There was so much horror to be imagined as we passed guard towers and signs with the skull and cross bones in front of what seemed to be miles of barbed wire.

The last stop on our grisly tour was the cremation room with one side devoted to gassing the prisoners while the other had large ovens to bake the once living human into more manageable proportions. All of us walked out of that room in some form of shock. Some people cried, others shook their heads but all of us were quiet.

Our guide took us back to our shuttle to be driven to Birkenau, officially known as Auschwitz II-Birkenau, not far down the road. The same drill was followed as we met with our counterparts, found our guide and made our way to the infamous Birkenau gate. We walked down the main road with the train tracks running parallel and came to a single cattle car. The guide explained how a man had the cattle car and it was the exact same model as what the Nazi's used to bring hordes of people from all over to that death camp.

Once they arrived the soldiers would order the people inside, some who had been traveling for days, to line up. The ones who were deemed able-bodied would be put to one side destined to spend the rest of their time in the camp under harsh working conditions while the ones who were lame were told they could clean-up after they walked to the end of the long road. What awaited them was death and our tour group walked the same road all those thousands of people had. The heaviness of that walk was hard to deal with as I thought of what they must have been hoping for, one last bit of humanity by being able to wash themselves and hope to get better and leave the torment they had not known they were succumbing.

At the end of the road we were met with a monument to the people of the camp. The train tracks ended there as well and poignantly someone before us had laid a bouquet of roses at there terminus a hint of beauty in a place which had seen so much death and exudes a somberness I had never felt anywhere else before or since.

We toured the living conditions of the prisoners, passed all the rubble which had been crematoriums and barracks. In some of the buildings left standing there were murals painted showing the last thing many of those people felt before they died, hope. The tour ended with the story of how those people were freed and the tales of them trying to get back to their old lives, a life that was far different from when they left it in a place that was mutilated by a relentless war.

All of us in the tour group thanked our guide and we walked back to our shuttle to be taken back into the real world. No one spoke on the trip back. My mind kept racing back and forth at what I had seen and I kept thinking how fortunate I, and the millions of tourists each year, were to be able to view the sites of one of the worst assaults on humanity history has ever known. I was grateful to have toured the haunting relic kept in tact and open for the whole world to tour, not for some gruesome exhibit into the macabre but instead a reminder to our species of the depths we can sink if our reality is twisted and our watch is down.

The shuttle dropped the three girls and I off in front of our hostel mid-afternoon and we all talked about how heavy the day had been. I walked around the town trying to get the feeling of reality back and try to come to terms with what we had seen. Normalcy set in only when I saw lovers holding hands with heads on shoulders and people on sidewalks smiling with beers in their hands and people in cars waving their hands at people driving poorly. We as a society are not perfect and never will be but what travel teaches is we, all over the world, are out for the same things. We want to be happy, do right by our family, provide for the ones we love and try to leave this world a little better than when we came into it.

    I stopped at a food truck and grabbed a humongous hot dog, bought a bottle of wine and retired back to the hostel for an early night. After a few hours the wine was empty and I had had a nice conversation with some people in the common room. We talked about travel and where we had been and where we were going. I climbed into my bunk that night amidst the snoring and low talking and thought of the people lost at Auschwitz. My eyes closed and I was happy I had the privilege of traveling and seeing things that startled me and pushed me to a point I hadn't known was near. I was happy to be living the life I wanted and I was happy to have plans to see so much more of that beautiful land they call Europe.

Chapter 10

Czechia

Autumn was in full swing in southern Poland and I was heading southwest. Like all of my mornings in the dank hostel in Krakow, it began started prematurely with the nasal-fueled goings-on of a large fellow across the room. With a train to catch I was thankful for the awakening, grabbed my things and hit the streets before seven. Grabbing my usual breakfast from a convenient market I made my way to the central station and boarded the first train. Surprised at how nice the train car was I sat back and read my new book while the orange and red leaves on the trees flashing by the window made me feel like I was in some kind of independent film.

After a bit of a layover I boarded the second train. This one was not nearly as nice as the first but decent as far as trains go. Traveling by train is such a romantic affair especially whilst traveling in Europe. Something about getting on a large mechanical snake and winding through the countryside watching the trees and houses and people flash by adds to the air of mystery of the land. There is no worry about where you are going because you are on rails and when a book is in your lap and coffee touches your lips and the car is rattling all is good in the world.

    The last layover was at a small town in the Czech Republic and I had forgotten they used different currency and I tried to buy a sandwich from a market and the lady gave me a questioning glance like this had never happened before. I exchanged a small amount of money and gave her the kind she wanted and boarded the last train. Walking on I found a seat and smiled at how nice the cabin was, it felt like I was sitting on an airplane. I made myself comfortable and began to relax when the ticket lady came by and asked to see my ticket. Scanning it with her eyes she politely told me I was in first class with a second class ticket and I had to go two cars ahead. Feeling a bit embarrassed I smiled, grabbed my things and went to the correct car. I was not alone.

    The car next to the first class one was the food car and the car after that was second class, it was completely full. There were people standing in the aisles in that car and people had spilled out into the connector piece between cars, some sitting while others stood. Being slow to realize it I finally came to the obvious conclusion they had oversold the tickets on the train to make more money and I had to stand. I tried to make the best of it and sit in the alleyway but whenever I did the waitresses had to walk to and from cars so I had to stand back up then down then up again until finally I stood the rest of the way to Brno.

The train finally made it to our destination and we all spilled out onto the platform each person zigzagging here and there in a frenzy. Hungry, tired and annoyed about the decreasing quality of train over the past few hours I found the trusty McDonald's logo, ate and used their Wi-Fi to properly locate my hostel. It had begun to rain as I walked out of the restaurant and made the trek to my hostel just outside the main square. Just as darkness began to set in I found my home for the next two days and ascended the stairs. As I was checking in I heard a deep bass thumping from below me. I must have looked questioning because the guy behind the counter told me the hostel was attached to a dance club, it was only a Wednesday so it shouldn't get too loud.

After securing payment he led me into a large open room with eight guys talking, playing cards and on their laptops. We all said our "hellos" and I was ready to choose my bunk when the guy began opening two large doors at the far end of the room. "No my friend, you are in here," he said and showed me in. The room was massive as far as hostels go and I had it all to myself. The front desk guy left me and I began unpacking and making myself at home.

The next morning I woke forgetting I had been alone in the room and not having been tormented by that incessant snoring of the previous days. On the train from Krakow I had decided to start a new writing regiment in order to make progress on a book I had started but not yet finished the previous winter. My idea was to have my fingers typing on the book each morning at eight and it was now ten 'til. I snuck past my sleeping comrades in the other room and placed my tablet on the table in the center of the kitchen. Words began to flow and I was happy.

Time flew by and an hour and a half snuck past me without feeling it as used to be sleepers from the room beside me came in for the morning coffee. We talked about what there was to do in Brno and not long after I found myself walking toward the city center with a vague idea of what my day held. I did my usual meandering up and down random city streets admiring the architecture of a new country and listening to the new accents I had only heard briefly on my way to the hostel the night before.

One of the strangest structures I had noticed since arriving in the town was a strangely phallic object near the center of the open public square. After talking to some of my hostel companions they told me it was an astronomical clock which looked like "a great big black dick!" Walking closer to it the guys were right.

Standing tall, maybe fifteen feet, the granite obelisk is definitely a strange sight. On the side of the giant thing there is a diagram on how to read the clock but only a couple of the many around the thing said they could actually read the time. It was about five to eleven when I was there and there was a large group gathering around the so-called clock. I asked a fellow American tourist what was happening to which he replied "I guess at eleven it shoots out a giant glass marble." The man shot me an unimpressed look and we waited for the big moment.

The clock struck eleven and everyone became giddy with anticipation. Soon a large glass sphere came clinking out onto the cobblestones and a young guy grabbed it and held it up with glee. I hurried over to get a closer look and wasn't too impressed but glad he was and the crowd dispersed everyone going their own way a bit disappointed but snickering. Music was playing in the square on the other end from where the astronomical clock was located and the Chinese flag was raised and dancing girls with hair pulled back into ponytails moved their bodies in synchrony with the music. They had food for sale and I bought soup and some ordure's and watched the dancing for a bit then continued on my random wanderings.

Soon I found the Sherlock Holmes Pub, a small English style pub with the visage of Sherlock Holmes with his Meerschaum pipe and deer stalker's cap positioned above the door. Feeling up for a beer and free Wi-Fi I found my way inside, ordered a large mug of dark beer and sat on the second floor.

Searching for things to do I found I was basically on top of Europe's second largest ossuary, interested I finished my beer and crossed the street to the Church of St. James. Near the base of the large church was a staircase with signs for the Brno Ossuary pasted all over it and I descended. I bought a ticket and grabbed the typewritten tour guide and walked amongst the piles of bones from some fifty thousand persons. The guide said their deaths ranged from the medieval plague to victims of the Thirty Years War.

The museum was arranged in a way which resembled a sort of labyrinthine shrine. The first stop along the tour was down a dank corridor with bones on all sides, candles lining the pathway and eerie music playing on speakers above. At the end of this macabre alley lay around fifty skulls stacked upward, some adorning holes upon their shining bone while others bore a deep red tinge. With no one else in the museum, the ambiance worked its magic and made me feel confronted with mortality, something easy to happen when confronted with a pile of skulls looking back at you. Turning around and heading toward the rest of the ossuary, I came into an open room with the bones arranged in a sort of vase-like column with gold statues of thin men scattered here and there. The gold tint of the lights in the room made the entire scene feel as it should, creepy and isolating yet not in a frightening way.

As I ascended back to the streets of the living I was glad to have stumbled upon the unique museum and it made me anxious to get to the Catacombs of Paris, one of the few things I had planned on seeing before I had even left America. While I was in the pub I also found the Brno Castle, or Spilberk Castle, was close to the market square. From its vantage point on the top of a tall hill I could see all around the city of Brno, not only its downtown area. Like so many times before I walked as far as I could until I was met with an entrance fee and backed off. I spent time photographing the beautiful trees in their full autumnal glow and took in the sights of the surrounding area.

Making my way back into the town square I heard more musicians playing. Some were groups of five with violins and cellos playing classical music while others were a kind of percussive marching band. Everyone sounded great and it was pleasant to see the youthful energy behind the shining instruments. I wandered around a part of town I hadn't yet explored and found a movie theatre playing some films in English and decided to keep with my trend of watching movies to give myself a bit of normalcy for a couple hours.

After the film I grabbed a Turkish kebap, bought a scarf and picked up a small moleskin notebook to keep note of stories I wished to write and a basic journal of events for posterity. I made it back to my hostel before too late and retired to my large empty room with only my thoughts and notebook to keep me company. I would be traveling south once my consciousness was lost to sleep and the new day came forth.

Travel is an interesting thing. When you start out, the sights are what you look forward to. After you get to the country you realize the culture is what is fascinating. Finally, once you settle into your hostel/hotel and start talking to others you find people are the reason travel is so worthwhile. The locals are the best. They are the ones who know the history of their city, they know what to see and what not to, and they are real, no bullshit just everyday people living their lives in which we, the tourists, are only fleeting. A close second to the locals as far as interesting goes are the other travelers. They are the ones with the amazing stories to tell because they are living their adventure. Whether that adventure is one of world travel or crisscrossing all over the place or if its living in a new country for a few months the idea of someone uprooting themselves for a dream and adventure will always move our gears of interest and intrigue.

After arriving to Prague I was stunned. The city is massive and it seems like every square inch is covered in beautiful architecture ranging from the darkest gothic to the elegant baroque. With only a vague idea of how to get to my budget hotel I took off with sparkling eyes. It felt like I was walking through a film set of black buildings with high points and the statues looking medieval in their form. Walking through the old town square I was engulfed by the overpowering architecture, the atmosphere was one of a different time.

 I stopped at the huge astronomical clock and stood admiring at the gold circles with statues painted beautifully adorning the face of the giant. Continuing along I passed under a tall black gate tower with green roof pointing to the sky in its gothic way. The Charles Bridge is as stunning as everyone says it is with the statues rising from its long-standing stones and street artists pocking the distances between them playing all manner of instruments and painting on canvas. Leaning against the edge of the bridge I looked out over the city with its red-tinted roofs standing magnificent against the beautiful blue sky of the day and thought of the wonder of the Czech people and the grandeur the people of Prague live in every day

 I made it to an open square next to St. Nicholas Church and took a deep breath, it was relieving to be out of the claustrophobic mess of tourists and street peddlers bombarding my every turn since I had arrived the busy metropolis. After checking-in I made my way to the room expecting to meet the same kinds of people I had been meeting the entire trip, young people my age with grand, but exhaustingly similar, stories of travel. The magnetic key I was given wouldn't work so I knocked on the door hoping someone was inside. There was an unintelligible response followed by loud clicking then the door swung suddenly open and a short Asian man with grey hair and wooden sandals was already walking away from the entrance.

Thanking him, I walked into the first room which was part kitchen, part bathroom and had two beds lining the opposite wall. With sore shoulders I threw my backpack onto an empty bed in the large second room and began unpacking.

"Where are you from?" The small man had clicked into my room surprisingly quiet and was looking down at me with interest.

"America, how about you?" I had learned along the trip it is better to play ignorant then assume someone is from a certain country.

"I am from Japan. I am traveling the world four years now." The English he spoke was quite good but his annunciation of certain words were overly strong while others slipped beneath.

"Wow!" I replied, impressed. "Why have you been traveling so long?"

"I worked in the government for many years and when wife died I had no reason to stay in Japan. I retired and started traveling. My retirement pays for my travels."

The progression of responses made me think he had been asked these questions so many times before. "That's a pretty great system, getting paid to travel. How much longer are you going to travel?"

"My goal is to visit the capital of each country in the world. I have been to many, but there are many countries in the world." The man hadn't moved much since we began talking. Sometimes he would alter his stance and put pressure on a different foot but overall it seemed like he enjoyed standing.

"That is quite an impressive goal. Have you been traveling with those wooden sandals the whole time?" I couldn't resist asking about his footwear. They didn't seem comfortable and I couldn't imagine wearing them all over the world.

"Yes. They are called Geta and they are traditional to my country. I wear them everywhere I go." The man took one of the sandals off and showed me how rigid the wood was and the leather thong on top which fit his foot just right.

The man with the wooden sandals and I talked for a while about where he had been and where his next country was to be. It was amazing how different his attitude was from all the other travelers I had met, myself included. Everyone before him was frothing with excitement at telling a stranger where they had been and what they had done in hopes the stranger could be benefited from or impressed by their nomadic frolicking around the world. The man with the wooden sandals was different. The man was modest, almost beyond so. Never did he boast about the dozens of countries he had been to, in fact it was only after much prying did I get him to talk about any of the places he had been in depth.

After talking more and more he showed me the pack he was traveling with and the sheer frugality of personal items within. Only basic toiletries, a small tablet, a few clothes and a journal had been all he carried for years now. The man reminded me of some kind of modern day monk traveling for enlightenment, not on a path to traditional religious enlightenment but a path down spiritual enlightenment with new experiences and new things being the guiding light.

Maybe that is why we all travel, at least all of us "westernized" travelers who seek something more than parties and sexual flings. I knew my reason for travel had morphed into a kind of quest to be totally away from my normal path. To not have to abide by any rules and to be free to do whatever I wanted, whenever I wanted. To wander the streets of the cities of the world and try to shed my tourist aura as much as possible and see the culture for what it is, a normal way of life in a different part of the world.

That night I went out and walked the streets of Prague. I saw the tourist attractions, stopped by the astronomical clock to celebrate its 605th birthday, saw the throngs of young people in skimpy dresses and button up shirts looking for the next big party on a Friday night while the Japanese man in the wooden sandals kept popping into my head. The trip he was on pervaded my every thought that night and the next two days spent in Prague. The simplicity with which he traveled inspired me and made me want to shed all of my previous thoughts of how backpacking through Europe should be.

Over the weekend our room was filled with three Russian guys in their mid-twenties and three girls the same age from Ukraine. All of us would talk and they invited me to club with them but they would look down at the Japanese man with sneers and laugh at his wooden shoes. Not once did they ask him his story or even try to understand where he was coming from. I declined their invitations and stayed in the small hotel writing late at night after exploring the city during the day alone and with walking tours.

While on the train still further south to the next city after two days in Prague I thought back on my time in the great city. I was glad to have wandered through her streets and to have seen those buildings but that felt secondary to the comparison of those young people I met with only hollow travel adventures next to the man who was totally alone in his own world with his own ambitions. Leaving Prague I was content for many reasons but the main was wrapped up in meeting the man with the wooden shoes and wondering where in the world he is.

I started calling myself a writer in České Budějovice, a town about two and a half hours south of Prague by train. The idea of being a writer has always fascinated me, in fact I almost committed to an English major in college but decided to get a degree in biology instead. I figured, I can read the same books and write as much as someone in college can without a degree and still put out my own books. That logic is correct but the truth of the matter is quite different. When writing, or participating in any form of art for that matter, is not your primary focus, like being a professional with it, it becomes easy to put on the back burner and not touch it for a long while. I was intent on changing that as the trip went on.

I had my journal open and my pen flowing sporadic across the pages jotting down ideas for writing projects as the the train pulled into the small station. I was relieved by how few people there were. Prague was congested at every corner with tourists and locals alike trying to get to where they wanted at all costs. České Budějovice felt different but not only because of the size, only 100,000 people strong, but mostly because of the accents. In so many of the large cities in Europe the first accents I heard were normally some variation of English. Whether they be American, Australian or from England the words would float around the rafts of people and pollute the feeling of being in a new place. The atmosphere of the city felt different.

With it still being early and only a short walk to my hostel I took my time to meander up and down the alleys and walk into bookstores and small cafes. Soon I found myself at the edge of the old town center. The multi-colored buildings formed a perfect square all around the large area with some bright yellow, others pink and situated in a corner of the square, the town hall painted a beautiful baby blue and built in the baroque fashion. In the center of the square sat a large fountain depicting Samson and his lion. Beautifully ornate, it is the largest fountain in the Czech Republic.

Passing through the square I turned down a curved alley and saw the sign for my hostel. Before I made it to Europe I had a picture in my head of what a hostel would be like. A bar or restaurant on the first floor with rooms on the second. This hostel completed the image. Opening the door I was greeted by a woman behind a traditional bar who spoke next to no English. We tried to have the "check-in" conversation but it was going nowhere fast. Soon a large man with a beard came to help us, I paid for my two nights then he showed me to a part of the wall opposite the bar which was a hidden door, or at least hidden from my view.

We ascended the stairs and came to an open room which split into two hallways. We took the left and came to a good sized dorm room with three bunk beds, a desk and a bathroom to the side. The man, who I came to know as Jan, told me no one had made reservations so I would more than likely have the room to myself for the next couple of days. Jan left and I was alone once again in a large dorm room in a different European town. I unpacked my things and went back outside looking for a grocery store. I found all the essentials a writer would need when hunkering down for multi-day writing bender; beer, energy drinks, and plenty of salty snacks.

As the light outside my window began to wane the bar below my bed was beginning to come alive. I heard people drinking at the bar, drinking in the room further into the establishment and drinking next to the stacks of firewood situated against the large fireplace crackling warmly. Jan came out from the smoke filled room and asked if I wanted to join him for a drink but I said "No thanks, I have some writing to catch up on" and I went back to my cold room. After a quick microwave meal I opened a tall can of cheap beer and began work on a novel. I had called myself a writer and writing is what I was to do. The words flew from my fingers at an astonishing rate. Taking sips from the beer can fueled my creativity and the laughs and yells in different languages below me set the mood and the world felt right.

Most of that first night was spent writing, the same with the next morning and into that afternoon. Feeling guilty about not leaving the warm room, I took a long shower and made my way down the stairs to explore more of the city. Jan gave me a tourist map and suggested places I should go and I left with the blue skies complementing the painted architecture of the city. After a couple of hours of wandering and a pint of the original Budweiser Budvar which makes the cities name famous I hurried back to the hostel to continue itching the writing bug which now pervaded my thoughts.

Like before, I walked into the bar with the laughter and the smoke and Jan pleaded me to join him for a drink and I agreed but first "I have to write." I spent the next three hours in a type-infused haze with words leaking from the pores of my fingers at a burning rate. With my head hurting from the concentration I made my way down the stairs, bought a beer, found a tall table next to the raging fireplace and scribbled in my notebook.

Before I could finish my beer the lady behind the bar who couldn't speak English came over with a shot of a brown liquid and pointed to Jan in the corner. I looked over and he raised his hand in a "cheers" and we drank together from across the room. Soon I was at his table with three other men of massive size with beards just as bulky and we drank more shots and more beers until finally it was last call and we all hugged like grown men do and I stumbled up the stairs. The bus south left in the afternoon and I was glad to have partied with a room full of Czechs and I reveled in them calling me "the American."

The morning came with a ferocity and a pain filled my head from whatever foreign liquor Jan and his friends decided to imbibe in from the night before. A long shower and an energy drink curbed the pain and I soon packed my things and descended the narrow stairs to check-out. The entire bar was black with chairs stacked and not a soul around only the smell of old beer and wood smoke left to remind me of the night before. I placed my key in the bin outside and trekked on for food.

After some last minute meandering to take in the feel of the quaint little town I made my way to the bus headed south and within half an hour we were in the charming hollow of Český Krumlov. The city was like walking through a postcard with a castle perched atop a hill and the architecture looking like a medieval movie. The postcard city was also quite small and walking around the entire old town district took less than an hour in which I found my hostel and was greeted by a wonderful woman who showed me to my room.

Within minutes I was back into the marvelous little town exploring here and there taking in the autumn air and loving the way the fog hung low around the castle and the pink church. Once night engulfed the scenery and cold rain began to fall I retreated back to my hostel and met my two roommates. They were two friends who had met at Oktoberfest, one was from Australia and the other from New Zealand. They were young guys and wanted to drink so we ran to a nearby market, bought cheap beer and spent the rest of the night talking about Australian football, rugby and how American football was full of weak men in overstuffed pads. The night went long and once we were done the single beds in the small dorm room were welcoming.

The following day was spent writing followed by exploring the area outside the tourist-filled old town while the rain would come and go. The ambiance of the small town fueled the creativity brewing in my brain so well and my two roommates asked me what I do and I would tell them "I'm a writer" and they would nod their heads and simply say "cool."

Working on the novel was rewarding but the acceptance of what I was doing in Europe began soaking its way into my psyche. I was living a kind of bohemian travelers dream with my only goal for the next couple months being to photograph the beauty I saw, write about the experiences I had, and travel to any destination I desired. There was no real long term goal for the photos or the writings, the only thing that mattered was to live in the moment and do exactly what I wanted to do each day.

    The day ended in a quaint traveler's restaurant in the middle of the old town with a large mug of pilsner, a warm fire drying my scarf and jacket, and my journal open with the possibility of the upcoming adventures. I would be in a new country the next morning and a new one the following day and a new one the third and the notion of fast travel overtook me as I was taking a drink from the tall beer and some dribbled down my shirt and I couldn't help but laugh out loud. Everyone in the restaurant was in the midst of their own travels and they didn't care. There was not a care to be had anywhere in that dim pub with a crackling fire and cold beer drank from large glasses, life was good.

Chapter 11

Three Countries

The car drove across the Czech-Austrian border without ceremony, actually we had crossed country borders without stopping at all. In the fog heavy morning of mid-October my driver, I say my driver because it was only he and I on the three hour excursion, drove on through the damp countryside. The driver was an early thirties high school (or European equivalent) history teacher with a wife and small child. For the first hour of our trek to Vienna we talked about our love of history, my education in biology, how close I had gotten to a family of my own, and why I was wandering around Europe instead of getting a good paying job. The conversation sputtered to a halt once we met an impasse between at the central theme of my adventure, it was too early to tell what it all really meant or why I had chosen to meander for such a long period of time without any real destination.

In what was beginning to trend toward normality, I was in a new country in the early morning without a clue where to turn and relishing every second. Vienna is gigantic. Not only that, it is sprawling and there is so much to see with little distance covered. Once my driver let me off on a sidewalk near the downtown area I swiveled on my heel, chose a direction which felt right and walked on. I soon found myself in the museum quarter and wandered. There was no real purpose to my walking except looking at old buildings with western tourists standing slack jawed with twenty year old headphones on their ears and socks pulled up a bit too high.

Not liking the vibe I turned and wandered the opposite direction. Every once in a while I would run across an opulent cathedral, next it would be a large building which had the feel of importance but since I had done none of my homework I had no idea. Towards the end of the day I found Schönbrunn Palace, a gorgeous Baroque on the outskirts of the city. Standing behind the luxurious fountain overlooking the pruned trees, red rose bushes, and sprawling grounds I began to think about my trip thus far.

Aimless wandering used to be fun, it was an exhilarating rush to come across something I didn't know would be there, it was as if I was discovering something. Yet, Vienna was a turning point for me. No longer was it enough to happen upon a beautiful building, take it in, then move on. I felt myself wanting more.

The coach bus drove along the motorway, underneath the legs of a UFO-shaped overpass, and down into the gutters of Bratislava where the bus load of young people unloaded looking interested and a tad bit unnerved. Some of the group seemed to know where they were headed so I followed them and we soon arrived at the base of a grand complex that was the Bratislava Castle. The same feelings of awe came over me upon seeing the castle. It was huge with four gleaming white walls all coming together at their edges in fortified buttresses. I climbed the steep inclined ramps and was soon overlooking the city of Bratislava with its red roofs and intricate old town.

After some photos, I descended from the castle and decided not to go immediately into the old town tourist district. Instead I found myself walking amongst the everyday houses and people going about their business, visiting delis and talking with one another amongst drinks on the sidewalks. It acted as a reset button to get away from the tourist districts and see how the normal people live in different countries. At the end of the day we are all the same and, essentially, do the same things. It was comforting notion and it felt in someway like I was going about my normal business back at home.

Throughout Bratislava a beautiful old town district jittered with lively bars and cathedrals, beamed with community art projects, and danced to the beat of street musicians. I indulged a bit in the night life before making my way to the hostel, getting a complimentary beer, and finding the hostel bar. It was a Monday so the bar wasn't busy and I drank with the bartender and talked about my travels and after a few drinks we were deep into European politics and how easy it was for drugs to cross country borders. After two blonde Russian girls entered the bar my drinking partner became preoccupied so I went up to my room which I thought would be empty.

Instead a young guy around my age in full motorcycle gear with the face of a male model was dripping water on our floor talking to a Canadian girl sitting atop the bunk adjoining mine. We drank cheap beers and talked about how the Canadian girl was solo tripping to Turkey and how the male model, who turned out to be a German living in Switzerland, was on a multi-country motorbike trip before he graduated college. We talked about our love of mountains and the German told stories of how he and his college friends climbed often in the Alps and he told me I *had* to try it sometime, especially if I was heading that direction, which I was, and to give him a call if I was ever in Switzerland and wanted to head out to the top of the Alps. Amazing the people you meet when traveling.

Morning came suddenly and my head was pounding. The constant go of travel and the late nights of mixing drinks and greasy food started to take a toll on my body. Trying to be quiet, I left the German motorcyclist and the intrepid Canadian traveller and walked onto the damp cobble stoned streets of old town Bratislava. I hunted down anything that seemed healthy, settling on a juice, tracked down the train station and bought a last minute ticket to Budapest.

Budapest is one of those cities I had always heard of but never had any ambition of actually visiting. On the train I thought back to all of the news I had been hearing about the refugee crisis and the stories of hordes of Syrian refugees camping out at the Budapest train station waiting, pleading, to get away from their country's strifes and enter a land with better prospects. Upon arriving at said train station there were no hordes of people looking desperate but the normal mixture of travelers. Leaving the depot there was a small contingent of Red Cross volunteers but the relief effort seemed much more controlled.

The rains had followed me to Budapest and with the night setting in I searched for my hostel. In the past the search was never much more difficult than marking a pin on a map and walking towards it. This case was different and after walking in circles for nearly an hour and with my eyes welling up with frustrated tears I walked into my hostel. A young man with white contacts, to give the effects of no pupils, and Emo-black hair helped me to my room where a young guy, my age, sat on his computer. The guy, James, and I hit it off instantly and talked incessantly about our travels. James was an Australian photographer who had decided to travel the world. We spent the night talking about all manner of things over cheap beer bought from the market below our hostel.

The following morning James and I decided we would explore the city together starting with a walking tour. The tour was great and we soon picked up a Brazilian girl, again our age, to join our cohort. Over the next several hours we explored all Budapest had to offer from museums, the old town district, the waterfront, cathedrals, and finished atop the city at the Budapest Castle. During out walking tour our guide told us about this particular Hungarian liquor which we found in the heart of the tourist district. Shots turned into beers which turned into bar after bar. The night spiraled into a drunken stupor which ended back at our hostel with a group of people talking about travel plans, the life they left at home, and an old Argentinian man eating rice and beans talking about how a person shouldn't travel quickly, should stay in one new spot for a few months to feel the culture, immerse oneself in the essence of the people making up the community. I told him about my travels, traveling to over a dozen countries in three months, what kind of travel did that teach? His head shook side-to-side slowly in disgust, "that is no way to travel *fully*."

That thought rang out through my head as I laid in bed that night with the spins. When traveling in hostels the introductory statements go as follows: where are you from, where have you been, where are you going? According to the old Argentinian man it doesn't matter. We are all on a journey somewhere and have started from an ambiguous place. Travel is just the act of getting from one ambiguous state of being to the other. What matters is the in-between, the journey, the part where stories are made, but according to him the most important stories are the ones gained by holding fast and digging deep beneath the surface level.

The past three days travel had been fast, ridiculously fast, three different countries in three days fast and I was to be heading back to Austria the following morning. My eyes opened in the pitch black of the room, everyone snoring around me as the Argentinian man's words rang through me, rattling every inch of consciousness I could muster.

What if he was he right?

Chapter 12

Austria

The hard wooden bench situated within the fortified walls of Hohensalzburg Castle was a welcome relief from a long day of travel. Due to the enforcement of a travel ban in Croatia, I had decided to avoid the region all together, very much to my disappointment, and push on to Austria. As I sat above the city of Salzburg looking at the dark clouds engulfing the Alps in the distance I contemplated what would lie ahead.

My entire vision of Austria was the alps. I've had a fascination with mountains for some time and have made my way up a few peaks in the Pacific Northwest but something about the history of the alps, whether they be Swiss or Austrian, held a particular vintage allure I couldn't place. There I was sitting in a beautiful 11th century castle in a picturesque city staring at the mountains in the distance wanting in some way to climb them, be a part of them. They stand for adventure, a kind of no-holds barred arena where man had gone to conquer the elements, had done so, and then made that which was once wild tame. That night at my hostel I searched for ways to get to the top of those jagged peaks. The answer presented itself in a brochure placed neatly in the dining area of the hostel.

The bus dropped me off at what seemed like the feet of Untersburg Mountain, a 6,500 foot snow-dusted craggy peak looming high above me with a cable car line running from where I stood and reaching far into the clouds above. With a smile on my face not felt since Iceland I bought a ticket to go up and stood in line with a young couple and their children. Before long we were on a cable car with a man and his dog as well as two older Austrian women, they all began to speak German while I braced the guard rails trying to ready my fear-frightened nerves for the ascent.

As we climbed higher in the car the women went quiet. The dog, a German shepherd with a stout muzzle, whimpered uncontrollably and went flat on the floor of the car having felt the altitude in the same ways my knees had. The view was breathtaking as we could see for miles in every direction while the fog still hid the higher peak of Untersburg and I began to feel better, taking photos to keep my mind off the height. The clouds suddenly broke and the distance from the cable car and the ground came rushing to my head with a panic, my knees shook, and the German women began whimpering in the same pitch as the muzzled dog. Luckily, the cable car terminal was near and our carriage shook its way into position, we all unloaded and went our separate ways, the majority of the car to the restaurant and me to the highest peak I could find; I was in the Alps.

It was -2 C (28.5 F) at the top of the mountain but the only thing that mattered was exploring. Trails wound in all directions and since it was late October there was hardly anyone up there. With my breath steaming all around me, I trudged up to what I thought was the peak, adorned with a large cross, and tried to look out over the Austrian countryside but was blocked by a thick cloud cover allowing me only to see the snow-dusted mountain scape. After a couple hours of hiking around I became discouraged by the thick clouds and decided to go down. The cable car wouldn't come back for half an hour so I decided to go into a hut perched on a ledge to pass the time, I was amazed upon opening the door.

The hut, Zeppezauerhaus am Untersburg, sits at 5,500 feet elevation and was built in the style of old alpine huts from the movies. A fire burned in a stone hearth and the bar was made of wood with character which had seen its fair share of harsh winters. The feel of the place was like something out of a classic mountaineers tale, I couldn't have been happier. I ordered a stein of German pilsner and a bowl of a hot soup I couldn't pronounce and began scribbling furiously in my journal while looking out the window periodically hoping for the sun to shine through.

After two steins the clouds began dispersing and I paid as quickly as I could much to the gaping eyes of the other other people, a family, in the hut. I was back to hiking up to the highest peak I could find and with the clouds parting I stood atop the Alps looking out over Austria a changed man living the dream I had set forth for myself before leaving my home country and undertaking such an incredible trip. I sat on a bench next to the large cross at the peak of Untersburg taking it all in, it was day 43 of my trip and I thought long on what I had seen so far and was amazed I was only half way through.

Early the next morning I left the beautiful city of Salzburg on a cheap bus to Innsbruck. My bus driver was a nice Turkish man who was fascinated at my way of cheap traveling and kept asking about the ladies I "had had" and what more was there to travel? Enjoying the small talk, I bantered back and forth with him until around a corner the Alps in their full glory appeared and stunned me into silence.

It was like something out of a magazine. The snow-capped range stretched onward for miles and my eyes couldn't be pulled away. My mind swam with all things "Alps" and as we neared Innsbruck the feeling of late October and my timing in the region couldn't have been better.

Once checked into my hostel I set out exploring the old town area with the Alps looming large behind multi-colored houses situated on the banks of a river. Arriving back to my hostel before dark I had been looking forward to a night of quiet and planning the next legs of my trip when a bearded man in his forties asked if I wanted dinner? Taken aback by his offer I asked why he would want to and he told me an interesting tale.

For decades he had been, and still was, a chef who had worked at high-end restaurants. Not liking to stay in the same spot for too long he had discovered the art of traveling from place to place funding this movement by cooking for people at hostels, charging them only for the ingredients then asking for a tip at the end which would be his profit. The man seemed trustworthy and was extremely nice so I agreed.

    The meal was absolutely amazing. Simple, healthy, and cheap but the taste was great and the cause was even better. By far the best part of the experience was the eclectic bunch of people at the communal dinner table. Travelers from Hungary, Israel, Spain, Poland, and Australia sat conversing with one another for hours, drinking cheap wine and talking of ways to make travel easier and where each of us were going and for how long.

    The camaraderie was palpable as we all helped clean up the dishes and gave our tips to the chef who had been smiling since we had walked into the room obviously proud of the work he was doing. After we all said our good nights I went into the common room with the rest of the hostel inhabitants and was met with a dull quiet. Everyone was on their phones and computers with headphones in tuning out the chance to engage with people from all over the world. Let down by the environment and overjoyed with indulging with the chef I climbed into bed early.

    Morning came with a shard of sunlight to my eyes from a crack in the curtain and I slowly rose to greet it. The Alps stood tall out of my window, it was paradise. After my customary morning writing followed by a cheap breakfast I found myself back in the old town district listening to more street performers and walking along the river taking in the Alps in the background. I had seen a sign near my hostel for a hiking trail and with the weather beautiful I listened to my instincts and followed the path.

After passing through a kind of adult jungle-gym, obstacle course I crossed some train tracks and ventured farther into the forest which seemed to grow more dense. Houses tucked away in these trees spotted the landscape until I came to a clearing and the trees gave way to rolling hills and the Alps presented themselves once again only somehow more prominent.

With excitement bubbling in all parts of me I trekked across the field, along old wooden fences and country homes until I found the extremely small town of Igls, I only knew it was called that from the sign above the vacant train station looking like it was from a movie set. The town seemed to be reserved for winter sports, a kind of rustic ski resort which I imagined would be quite busy in its peak season. Walking around the town I imagined what it must have been like in the past, even in 2015 it seemed to hold some of its old charm.

Hiking back to Innsbruck I thought of the next leg of my trip. It was exhilarating not having an itinerary to follow, just my own wants and desires to be my guide. That night I made the decision to travel into Switzerland and keep exploring the Alps. Everyone I talked to couldn't stop raving about how beautiful the country was and how much it had to offer. While curled up in my bed that night my roommate, an eighteen year old Australian, and I began talking of our travels. Once we had chatted for a bit I asked her where she had come from to which she responded Amsterdam.

Apparently she had spent a few days there partying, eating speed and MDMA, until she woke up next to her new boyfriend. The two of them had scored enough drugs in those few days to make some money selling them and before long they had either used the drugs themselves or sold them to junkies in need. The day before our talk she awoke having chewed her lip so bad when sleeping they were large and she had scabs on her arms. The boyfriend had gone and she was left with little money. She decided to travel to Austria for a few days to clean up before making her way into the cheaper countries of southeastern Europe where the remaining money could go farther.

As the girl spoke I began to notice the signs of abuse she had done to her body. The stories were raw and told with such a matter-of-fact attitude that I couldn't help but nod my head and give a forced grin. That night after the lights had been turned out I couldn't stop thinking about that girl sleeping feet away from me. Travel is, in some form or another, a way of escape. Escaping the daily grind of monotony, escaping the path we were destined to walk, or, in her case, an escape from whatever demons plagued her life, the same demons who kept finding her and dragging her back down. Sleep met me with the thoughts of escapism rambling through my skull asking the same question over and over again…what was I trying to escape?

Chapter 13

Italy

The sun woke me early from my bottom bunk and once my eyes cleared I could see the Austrian Alps out of my window and couldn't help but smile. Before long I was walking through the morning chill toward the train depot and realized clocks all over Salzburg were an hour behind mine. Still in my morning daze I shook it off and only upon being handed my train ticket did I fully accept the time difference. With a quick internet search I realized Europe dealt with Daylight Saving Time on different days than the US; all of the Austrian clocks were correct and I was not.

The train pulled into the station as punctual as I had grown accustomed, I found a vacant compartment, and we were off on our voyage to Italy. In the year before embarking on the trip I had taken notes of places people recommended, ranking them by the enthusiasm each felt and the stories they told. One of the top three was "take a train through the Alps" and as the train rumbled alongside those very Alps my mind began fluttering with what was to come.

With luck still on my side, my compartment had remained empty allowing me the full use of each seat, both coffee trays, and unimpeded access across the hall to the large side window. I took advantage of all of it and as we traveled through the mountains I raced from side to side taking photos, pressing my face against the window like a child, and watching the Austrian countryside slide past like a film. There were small towns with expansive bridges, churches placed elegantly by themselves with nothing around, and snow-capped peaks reaching jagged toward the blue sky all gleaming and glistening in the chilled air ready for my eyes to take them in.

After many interesting stares from my fellow passengers I decided it best to settle in to my cabin and take a break from my canine-like treatment of their lands. The rocking of the train and the chance to spread out uninterrupted was too much for my tired head to handle and I was soon asleep. In what seemed like a few minutes I woke and through rubbed eyes looked out the window of the still moving train. The landscape was entirely different.

What used to be sharp mountains gave way to vineyards sprawling across rolling hills. Grays turned to greens, stone to grapes, and the architecture smoothed and looked relaxed in comparison to its neighbors to the northeast. Italy was upon me and it was obvious, obvious in a way that both stunned and awed me.

The people who were boarding the train had also changed considerably. Skin grew darker and hair wavier. Women who were once bundled in coats and pants transitioned into flowing dresses. A young woman with black hair and everything I had expected Italian to sound like entered my compartment and we talked about where we each were heading. After silence met the two of us I caught myself staring out the window at the encroaching water. Like a kind of mirage, the water came closer and clearer, buildings began to appear and before I knew it the city of Venice was within sight. With a feeling like that of the Denmark to Germany travel, the train was cruising atop a bridge over water. With a halt the occupants of the train slowly marched off, I went through the train terminal, and found myself looking out over what could only be described as beautiful madness.

Venice was full of life. Water from canals was splashing upon walkways with the passing of gondolas carrying travelers of all nationalities. People were absolutely everywhere following along walkways going over small archways, in and out of corridors between buildings which seemed so old and many of them leaning to a noticeable degree. Tugging on my backpack straps and guessing which way my hostel lay I turned left, entered into the throng of lost tourists and shuffled.

I had never seen anything like it in my life. It was like being in a foreign film. The canals were how I pictured them, the people, the buildings, the accents, the chaos; it was like it should have been, quintessential Venice. Not caring about time I let myself wander. If I got tired of following the crowd I would turn down a random alley and take in the daily life of those who lived in that weird chaotic paradise. More than not I was met with a dead end due to the walkway leading to water, I turned around, entered the pack of people and kept walking.

Before long I was in the middle of the city at Piazza San Marco with thousands of people. The buildings were beautiful but I couldn't appreciate it with all the people shouting and posing for photos and bumping into one another. Frustrated, I got to the side of the square and tried to get my bearings. With a little luck I found directions on where to head and left the throngs of people thinking what a labyrinthine brute Venice was and was grateful upon finding my hostel situated directly over canals in the heart of the city.

The hostel was in a superb location but was cheap which meant the inside was not the best but it didn't matter, I was going to sleep above the canals of Venice! Darkness was upon the city and as the crowds began to die down I ventured out to try to find something to eat. Without much hassle I came across a small wood fire pizza spot with Italian men bickering between themselves, I ordered a pizza, found a cheap bottle of wine next door, and was soon consuming both at a frantic pace while sitting above the canals with the perfect Italian autumn breeze wafting music, accents, and the smell of food from all directions.

I sat there and took in the magic of it all. That morning I had woken up in the shadow of the Austrian Alps and with only a train ride I had transported to an entirely different world. That is what cheap travel is all about. It isn't about comfort or spending money on gourmet foods or expensive hotels, it is about living like some kind of homeless drifter, staying at the cheapest hostels, suffering through the worst transportation all so we can see as much as possible and live as much as we can, squeezing every ounce of life from each minute of the day, not taking anything for granted and experiencing as much as we can. The bottle of wine went down smooth and the pizza fast, how lucky was I to be living in that moment, taking it all in and wanting more.

The second day in Venice started early at a coffee shop next to a canal. In great comparison to the previous month in the north, Italy was warm and the sun shine thawed me out to great benefit. I watched people go about their day, young lovers holding hands basking in the romance of the city, and old men on boats cursing at each other in Italian.

Wandering through the city I tried to avoid areas with the most people. Gondola operators laughed jovially over cigarettes, street hagglers barked at tourists, a peculiar old man ran a bookstore as water splashed up from a canal, and people sang from the innards of all manner of shops; it was a kind of paradise to be an observer of such a fascinating life. Night came in the same way as before and I ate pizza over the canal while a bottle of wine soon disappeared.

Bologna is a city quite different from Venice but not any less interesting. Having been dropped off in the business district I walked through a typical big city scene to get to my hostel. Upon arriving, a little old Italian woman who was extremely kind and spoke broken English showed me my room. It was a lively hostel, much in the same way the hostel in Gdansk, Poland had been. Young people were talking, laughing, sharing stories about their travels, it was fun and maintained my euphoria after leaving such an exhilarating place like Venice.

After a bit of research I set out looking for the sights around Bologna. I passed the Towers of Bologna, walked around the Piazza Maggiore, and looked up at the Fountain of Neptune which all impressed me but soon I tired of the crowds around the sights and wanted to find an English bookstore. Unlike the cities previous, Bologna is a university city with a booming intellectual scene and because of this bookstores are quite easy to find. On my way to the first on my list I began noticing flyers posted on walls with revolutionary symbols. As I got closer to the university district they grew more numerous and once I entered into a square in the heart of the district students were in pockets with signs in Italian but with enough symbolism I could make out what the point was; revolution. Not fully understanding, but also not feeling threatened, I searched the bookstore and went back to my hostel intrigued by the scene.

That night the hostel kitchen was busy with all of its occupants gathered with cheap wines and meals made from scratch waiting to converse. At one point we all went around the room with a sheet of paper and wrote down where we were from. In the end there were ten of us and eight nationalities (Chinese, Turkish, French, Australian, Slovakian, Spanish, Argentinian, and me). The night raged on with each of us sharing our wine and beer, food and desserts, stories of travel and ideas on religion and politics, the revolutionaries and anarchists of the university, and what it meant to be alive.

Magic happened in that small hostel kitchen, a magic I will never forget.

My second day in Bologna acted as a rest day. Its the kind of day most travel blogs and books don't talk about. Laundry, emails back home, sorting through photos, chatting with friends, and venturing only as far as the nearest market for meals. Not exciting days but when traveling for months they are needed.

The third day started slow. A few girls were having a rest day after having traveled from the west of Italy and we talked about what there was to see from our experience. Without hesitation they told me to visit the Cinque Terre region along the northwestern coast, they assured me I wouldn't be disappointed. Jotting it down in my notebook, I ventured out back down to the university district, grabbed some pizza and headed back for an early night at the hostel. One of the people who was most talkative from two nights previous, an early thirties Turkish guy with a gloriously thick and well-groomed beard, asked me if I wanted to join his friend, a Turkish girl about my age, and some others at a bar for drinks. Trusting the guy I obliged and we walked to the bar.

The bar was like any bar, we got drinks and sat on the sidewalk in the warm autumn air. Before long, three Italian guys in their late twenties sat down, they introduced themselves to me, and the conversation took off like an explosive. As soon as they found out I was American they started asking questions, not in any kind of aggressive way but in the way college intellectuals converse with one another. I hadn't engaged in talks like that for some time and it lit a fire under my ass and we talked about all manner of politics, religion, the Italian president, the American presidential candidates, and, in what seemed their usual main topic, anarchy.

Without outright saying it, the three Italian guys were anarchists who didn't like the way their country was being ran and they were eager to protest that view as loud as they could. They talked about their weekly free dinners for the city, free concerts, clothing donation boxes, and the charity they were doing through the university. The guys were radicals but they seemed to have good heads on their shoulders and I was intrigued by them.

After a couple beers the guys asked if I wanted to join the group for a late night concert. The cute Turkish girl grabbed my hand and tugged on it, I couldn't resist, the conversation I had just took place in was amazing. The six of us walked through the lamp lit streets, through bad looking neighborhoods, across railroad tracks and bridges, and finally came to what could only be described as a punk rock charity center. A loud, clanky punk band was roaring on stage and people of all different styles were walking around with beers and food. We found a table and the Turkish girl asked if I was hungry. She left and brought back noodles with white sauce and a beer, I tried to pay her but it was free, one of the community events put on by whatever organization the anarchists were a part of.

Our group joined a bigger group and we all started talking about the same things as before. Looking around I was the only American at the venue, it was the first time the idea had really came to my head. I didn't feel threatened but felt welcomed. The conversation was so rich and the people I met were smart, organized, and passionate. The kind of people who really could change the world.

At around two in the morning, and after numerous beers, my two Turkish friends and I walked back to the hostel. We talked about our plans for the future, the lives we each had back home, how interesting it was we all had met and were in that one place at that one time. It was a strange night and probably the most intellectually stimulating of my entire trip.

My first impression of Florence was not great. The bus from Bologna had been an hour late and the drive, although short, was uneventful and traffic was congested. Once off the bus I was met with throngs of tourists and vendors and all I wanted was to get to my hostel to relax; it was one of those days. Even when on the trip of a lifetime and in the seat of Tuscany a traveler still experiences the blues.

    Meandering through the streets I took in the warm weather and blue skies, the shops with amazing smelling food, and eavesdropped endlessly on the multi-ethnic chatter of tourists all around me but I couldn't shake the feeling of not being impressed. I had expected so much from the seat of the Renaissance, the home of the masters. Just as my head began to lower from fatigue I saw it. Like some kind of medieval skyscraper that stood alone in its square jutting up in all directions with a shining white stone traced with reds and greens, topped with a giant dome which gave the complex its name; the Duomo or the Florence Cathedral.

I hadn't noticed but my mouth was agape, literally, in the stunning magnificence of the building. Reinvigorated with excitement I walked around the complex a couple of times then set off in a different direction, it didn't matter which. In quick succession I walked through the statue laden corridor of the Uffizi Gallery with the great thinkers on either side, came out overlooking the Ponte Vecchio (a bridge complex from the Renaissance era), turned and stood gaping at the Piazza della Signoria with its fountain dedicated to Neptune, replica of the David plus a myriad of statues strewn about like common bushes or lawn ornaments. It was embarrassing how unimpressed I was only an hour before and now I stood in the heart of Tuscany looking at architecture that was as mind blowing as anything I had seen until that point.

Every inch of that city is astounding but with dusk nearing I wanted to get high. It had become a kind of goal upon the arrival to each new city, get to the highest point possible, without having to pay which normally meant a natural area, and take in the view. Florence was no different and soon I was standing at the Piazza Michelangelo with musicians playing softly, another reproduction of David standing tall in the center of the square, and the city lights twinkling in the calm sunset of late October.

Morning came and a quiet coffee shop near my hostel helped ready me for the day. I had not realized it before coming to Florence but Pisa was only a quick train ride away. Taking a detour through the Uffizi Gallery, trying to find the statue of Leonardo da Vinci but failing, I made my way to the bustling train terminal. The train was late, as was normal in Italy, but soon we were in Pisa. I followed the herd of tourists through the shopping district, across the Arno River, and into the Pisa Cathedral complex. All of the pictures I had ever seen of the Leaning Tower of Pisa have shown only that, so when I stood at the entrance to the complex and noticed there was an entire cathedral in addition I felt beside myself with embarrassment. Tuscany was breaking all kinds of long held beliefs for me, beliefs that I realized were based on tourists traveling to foreign lands, taking a photo, then using that one image to define an entire region.

As expected, people were strewn everywhere. Most were with a group, each person trying to get the most unique photo of themselves posing with the leaning tower, usually stumbling from the difficulty but having a great time. After walking around the complex being sure to give the cathedral its fair amount of time I came back to the tower, took a few selfies, then wound my way out of the area smiling in the blue skies with all the rest of the tourists.

Not wanting to just come to Pisa for the tower, I strolled along the Arno River, meandering through some ruins spread throughout the city, and ate pizza at a local restaurant. Making my way back to the train station I started seeing people dressed in costumes, it was Halloween. Back in Florence more and more people of all ages kept popping up with different masks and outfits, some were children others were my age, all were out having a great time. I celebrated the day with a bottle of cheap wine back at my hostel talking to fellow tourists, ending the night looking into the Cinque Terre region everyone kept bringing up.

My last day in Florence was full of wandering around taking as much of the city in as possible. Tiring of the main areas I ventured off into the residential region and beyond to places where I could look one way and see the Duomo and the rest of the inner city but looking the other way see Tuscany in all of its beauty. Trying to circle back, I came across a large fort complex and soon realized it was free admission. The Forte di Belvedere can only be described as sprawling and the next couple hours were spent traversing its grounds which included the Giardino di Boboli (the gardens), its statues, and fantastic views of the taller buildings in the city center. I was amazed to find it and spent my time looking out at Florence, ready to leave but not ready to say goodbye.

Morning came at 4:30 as my hard-partying roommates snored below me. The cold air sent chills as I walked through the streets which had been so busy in my times on them before. Drapes of gypsy carts who had been selling cheap goods from street corners waved ethereal in the wind and the Duomo square was deserted save for a policeman and a drunk stumbling on the other side. The train station was alive but anemic and my train was late as usual. Trekking along the coastline in the early morning hours dissolved any animosity I had had about waking up as early as I did. Coastal cities passed by decreasing in size as the rocky shoreline began being dotted with colorful buildings in the distance.

With few people left on the train we arrived at Riomaggiore, a quaint coastal town built on a hill with pastel colored buildings bursting on either side of a main walkway. It was like walking through a postcard from a time long ago. There were no vehicles, the crowds hadn't arrived yet, local vendors were beginning to start their days with sandwich boards and Italian chattering and laughing. Without much difficulty I found my hostel and was walked through a labyrinth of alleys, steep steps, across a courtyard, and into an apartment style room. Intrigued by the layout of the city I quickly found my way down to the blue water with rocks jutting out into it and people lazily lounging in the morning sun.

Grabbing only the essentials I left my hostel and wound my way back through the alleys and onto a train bound for the northernmost city in the Cinque Terre region. Monterosso feels much more like a resort city as opposed to the fishing village vibe Riomaggiore gives off. None the less, the weather was superb and I trekked around the city for a bit before getting anxious about what lie ahead. Numerous people had told me to hike the Cinque Terre trail and after much reading I understood why. Linking the five villages (Monterosso, Vernazza, Corniglia, Manarola, and Riomaggiore) is a trail skirting along the rocky cliffs of the Ligurian Sea. After looking at all the pictures and hearing the personal stories I bounded up the steep cement steps ascending above Monterosso beginning the hike.

The one thing missing from my backpacking adventure had been nature. Back home I am an avid hiker and all-around lover of the outdoors. It is rare for me to go long periods of time stuck in a city before I go stir crazy and have to see trees, mountains, or an ocean. Besides a few exceptions (notably Iceland and the Alps) I had been confined to the cityscapes of some of the finest destinations on the planet. Yet there, cruising onward from Monterosso with the ocean air in my lungs and the alien, to me at least, Italian landscape all around I was in the zone. It seemed like every few feet I would have to stop and look at the cacti, take a photo of some new angle of the trail, or admire the diversity of people hiking along with me, luckily quite few were on the trail that day.

I came around a bend and saw Vernazza spread out below me. With the area's characteristic yellows and pinks adorning the buildings, a curving arm of rocks protecting its bay from the sea, and a tower perched above the city was in great contrast to the bright blue water surrounding it. Dipping into Vernazza I darted down a few alleys before ascending on down the trail. Vineyards sprawled across the hill sides with their winding branches stretching, intertwining with one another in a way which seemed so…Italian.

The sky was at its peak of the day and the heat baked the stone steps of the trail and sweat soaked through the beanie I was still wearing. It was probably because of that red wool cap in the ridiculous heat that people would pass and first smile their friendly way then glance above my eyes and furrow their brow if only slightly. Nothing mattered, the heat, the people, the views, it was all bliss as my hiking boot wrapped feet flew freely across the trail relishing in the stretching and climbing, dirt then streams of water and back to blistering stone.

Small shacks, which looked to be used for wine production, dotted the landscape, coming into arms reach at random points along the trail. I couldn't help but crane my neck to look into the alien buildings with their rusted conveyor belts and hooks and grape stained buckets. The buildings were rustic with their stoned walls and antiquated roofs and thin, old windows fragile enough to break at the slightest touch. The grapes on the curled vines were shriveled and their leaves yellowed and spotted with age lending a foregone beauty and fleeting want of a time only weeks previous when those branches yielded such wonderful juices.

Afternoon began to wane and the heat began to dissipate as I descended into the final enclave of residents along the Italian shores. With a backpacking travelers wallet I couldn't afford any of the wealthy tourist prices and stood longing at the windows of shops and fancy bars with enticing offers for classy drinks with clever names. Instead I wandered briefly along the cobbles and the pastel colored buildings, took in the stunning views, and watched the bobbing of small boats in the harbor before ascending the steep trail and trekking across the trail for the final leg.

Without realizing it, or better said, without looking closely at the map in my back pocket, I came to a sign which told the trail visitors the final leg of the trail was closed due to a landslide. An arrogance overtook me and I thought, if only briefly, that assuredly *I* could find a way around this impasse but within a few steps I was found to be only human and had to descend to the train station like everyone else.

Along the way I ran into a girl from the Bologna hostel, one who had recommended the very trail I was on, and we talked about how she had gotten to Cinque Terre and she introduced me to a few friends she had made and had begun traveling with. Our new group walked to the train station, the one connecting all five of the small towns together, and waited for our ride back toward Riomaggiore.

Our group talked for awhile about travel and where we were staying and how long we would be in Italy and how we should add each other on social media and meet up sometime later on our journey. With the sunset cast aflame along the horizon the group dispersed, the others to take selfies in the nirvana we found ourselves while I walked toward the shore to try to capture even a fraction of the beauty nature dealt out so effortlessly. The train beckoned and everyone grabbed their heavier-than-they-started packs and kicked off the trail dust from their shoes before dragging their exhausted bodies onto the locomotive. Upon seeing the landslide sign I had been pissed at not being able to walk the entirety of the Cinque Terre Trail but once the train jolted forward and we were floating along the rails of that Italian oceanside with the sunset a slight sliver and my feet humming with a dull pulse I was content with the outcome and glad to have experienced what the day had brought.

I arrived back to my hostel in complete darkness and was glad to see no one else had taken up residence on any one of the three bunk beds. Having explored my dining options before leaving for the trail I knew the isolation mixed with the exclusivity of the area meant everything was going to be ridiculously expensive. Instead, I ducked into one of the locally run markets, grabbed cheap red wine from the local vineyards and two pizzas for the oven.

With feet still sore from the hike, I hobbled through the narrow passages of the town, between stone embankments, across a roof top, and up the tight flight of stairs to my hostel. The cork popped on the wine bottle and a paper cup was filled to the brim as I clicked on the oven. I heard the gas burning within but there was no flame. Drinking down my paper cup of wine I threw the oven pizzas in the microwave, set a random time, then sat on the bed with a refill of red elixir and semi-cold pizza pouring over a map of Italy and loving life.

As midnight approached I had spilled wine on my map, wrote a few paragraphs in my journal, and edited a dozen or so photos. The wine was gone and so was the pizza, the Cinque Terre Trail had been hiked, and one of the most amazing sunsets of my life capped a day full of adventure and beauty. Once again I was doing what I had sought out to do on the adventure through Europe; to see as much as possible, learn as much as possible, and be Present every… single…day.

Sleeping in the next morning I woke to blue skies and an urge to get high. Pulling out my wine ring stained map of Cinque Terre, I noticed a winding trail reaching away from the main tourist trail, high above Riomaggiore. Packing a light lunch, I hurried up the steep incline through the vineyards and marshy bogs to a pink church overlooking the city and down the coastline. It was quite astonishing the contrast between the jagged rocks jutting from the turbulent ocean and the pastel colored buildings situated in a seemingly random placement. Hiking this way and that in the blue sky for hours I looked to the sea and saw grey clouds forming, heading my way.

Back in Riomaggiore there was a crowd gathering outside a small church with a hearse. A group of maybe thirty mourners wiped tears from their faces and marched behind the hearse as it ascended the cobbled street. I stood off to the side not wanting to make eye contact with any of the group but sometimes doing so and seeing sadness and I felt so out of place. There I was intruding on their city, on their day when a loved one passed and I was there without a care doing exactly what I, and only I, wanted to do.

The sun set that night in a tumultuous way, using the grey clouds to its advantage and scattering its beams. I sat on the edge of the village, near the water, thinking about what the trip meant to me. Everything was happening so fast and I was seeing so much that it was hard to wrap my mind around it all. The funeral got me thinking of mortality and my mind-in-the-clouds demeanor was forcefully brought back to the ground. I didn't really know what I had learned along the trip thus far nor what I hoped to gain from it in the time to come.

The sun greeted me the following morning while on a train to Genova, the thoughts of the night previous still casting gloom on my tired brain. Without much energy I found my hostel and did the usual. Talked about traveling with roommates, met a girl from California who wanted someone to walk around the city with, we chatted and traveled to the Genova Lighthouse, got pizza and wine, brought it back to the hostel and indulged in a long conversation about politics and travel with the rest of the hostel folk.

The funeral in Riomaggiore affected me in a way I couldn't shake. Everything seemed trivial, the boasting of where each person had been and where they were going, the superficiality of the girl from California, even the pizza seemed contrived. I was in a bad space going to bed that night ready for a change.

Not wanting to train from Genova to Barcelona I instead found an overnight ferry across the Ligurian sea. Walking along the docks taking in the giant ship my mood was back to being on high. The point of travel is to see things differently, explore, chase adventure with a reckless abandon and find new ways to pursue those things. Standing at the loading area of the ship an Italian officer took my passport and told me I would get it back in Spain. It was a bit alarming giving up my passport, my identity, to a stranger for that length of time but it didn't matter. I ascended the cramped stairway leading up the multiple stories of the small city on the water until I reached its highest point, the windy top deck overlooking the city of Genova.

The ship sounded its horn and we made our way out of the harbor steaming headlong into the Ligurian Sea bound for Spain. Like always, I had chosen the cheapest possible mode of transport which meant no cabin and no bed. Instead, I was to sleep with the other miscreants in the theatre room using the plush red chairs as a sleeping apparatus. Once I found the chair to my liking, and claimed it by tying a sleeve of my jacket to one of its arms, I roamed the ship taking in the unique environment.

Perhaps eighty percent of the passengers were of African descent, most it seemed were Moroccan and the rest belonging to the rest of the north coast of the continent. The dining area was a smorgasbord of characters. Some tables held dark skinned men playing cards shouting loudly at one another, others sat Italian bikers with leathers and patched arms crossed looking intimidating, women held children, some smoked on the bow of the ship, others drank beer after beer from the fully stocked bar, I sat in a corner with my notebook jotting all of this drinking deep from a bottle of cheap Italian wine I had packed.

With night upon us I ventured back to my red plush chair. The hallway floors were littered with dark skinned feet sticking out of blankets, most snoring loudly others twisting and scratching in their sleep. Men were walking around in their underwear with towels draped over their shoulders and some were on their knees praying quietly to themselves. A similar scene was taking place in the theatre room, I found my red "bed", tied my backpack tightly to my wrist and laid across two of the chairs shutting my eyes. The night was long and sleep escaped me for most of it.

At 6:12 an announcement came over the loudspeaker notifying us we were going to make land soon. I made my way to the main lobby and noticed a ten fold increase in the amount of white faces I had not seen before. It seemed those people with white faces were the ones who could afford, or at least were the ones who saw fit to purchase, the cabins. They were also the ones who avoided the common areas for I had walked every inch of that ship the night before and hadn't seen many.

The elevator doors opened and we all funneled in, colors of skin and nationality not mattering and we descended to the bottom decks. We were given our passports but only a fraction of the ship's occupants walked onto the docks. As we got onto our shuttle I looked back at the ship and many dark faces clutched the railing of the ship at her top decks, they were looking down on us and us up at them. The ship was bound for north Africa and so were they for whatever reasons. Our shuttle took us to the end of the harbor, I got off and walked amidst the shadows of palm trees in the early morning air of November, I was in a new country and my mind was set on traveling north.

PART III

HOMEWARD

Chapter 14

Spain

The sun was shining and the sky was blue as I walked past the many palm trees which lined the harbor and along the walkway making my way into Barcelona. At first there were few people around, it was early morning after all, but as I walked farther away from the harbor the amount of people increased until I turned at the Christopher Columbus pillar and found myself immersed in a huge group of people walking along the main tourist street within the heart of the city known as La Rambla.

A cacophony of accents, laughter, and shouting hit me head-on as I made my way past the talented street performers. With the lack of sleep from the night previous my senses, and tolerance, was frayed and before long I ducked into a fast food restaurant for black coffee and Wi-Fi in order to get my bearings. Sitting at a window seat overlooking La Rambla I watched as the stream of people flowed steadily along, everyone smiling and looking jovial in the morning beauty of the artistic city.

With many hours left until I could check-in to my hostel I did my usual wander by turning down random alleyways in search of interesting architecture and landmarks. Soon I found myself in a medieval looking area and came across a free walking tour of the city getting ready to begin. I asked if I could join, they obliged, and we were off.

The guide was a native Spaniard from the region of Catalan, of which Barcelona is at its center. With a neatly trimmed beard and thick rimmed glasses he could have fit in perfectly back home in the Pacific Northwest. Knowledgeable and full of interesting facts, the guide told stories, made us laugh, picked out the Americans from the crowd to banter with, and lead us to many historical landmarks across the city. The three hour tour ended down near the Arc de Triomf and the Parc de la Ciutadella. A few of us asked him what he recommended we must see on our varying times of staying in the city, he was nice enough to make us each a personal list, we tipped him well for his troubles, and the group split in our different directions.

It was nearing the check-in time for my hostel so I walked along the palm tree lined walkway, through the Arc de Triomf and on through residential areas and buildings adorned with little pieces of artistic flare, of which I was to grow accustomed in the expressive city. The area down along the tourist district was clean and gleamed with an affluence but as I neared my hostel the area descended into sketchiness. The hostel looked more like a hotel than those previous but I was glad since there would be an actual bed to lay my head as opposed to the reclining chairs I had used on the ferry.

Only accepting cash at the lobby, I reached into my pocket for the fresh 50 euro note I had just withdrawn but couldn't find it. A cold sweat came over me. I apologized to the front desk who was completely apathetic to my plight and scampered out frantically to retrace my steps. After half an hour of frantically searching I gave up, defeated from the hit my budgeted bank account would take, found a different graffiti laden ATM, and went back to pay for the hostel. Anger and frustration filled me, how could I have simply lost that much money in such a short amount of time.

I made it to my room which was dark and cramped with a young lady passed out, hair askew and snoring, atop one of the bunk beds. Throwing my pack on a bed I pulled out what I needed and stuffed the rest in a small locker. In no time I was back on the streets wanting to walk off my frustration. I made it back to the downtown area and walked through the streets as night began to set in admiring the numerous murals painted on the walls, enjoying the architecture, eating some cheap food, then walking along a harbor with sailboats bobbing up and down.

An English cinema was nearby and I caught a show then emerged afterwards in complete darkness. I had underestimated how sketchy the area my hostel resided actually was. As I walked back I kicked myself for not doing enough research but made it back. It turned out the hostel drew quite a few young people, as in barely drinking aged people, and was big into partying. I found the kitchen area, opened the bottle of wine I had bought from the market across the street, and wrote until late.

The next morning I settled into a small cafe and drank a latte while reading a newspaper. I took Spanish in junior high and high school but never had a chance to use it in everyday life. In the next two weeks of being in Spain I told myself I would get better at it. Once I left the cafe I noticed how hot it was and wanted to buy some sandals. I found a Chinese market and bought some cheap flip-flops and headed to the white sandy beach on the edge of the city.

I had done little research on Barcelona before I arrived and was astonished at the beach scene it had to offer. The water was dark blue and the sand warm in the mid afternoon sun. Taking off my sandals I walked eagerly through the crunching sand looking around at the tanned bodies of those around me contrasting sharply with that of my pale white skin. I sat in the sand at the edge of the washing surf watching people splashing around having fun. Out of the corner of my eye I saw a mid-thirties woman stand up and take of her bikini top and walk out into the water. I was stunned. It wasn't that I was opposed to being in the presence of a naked body, it was just…I wasn't expecting it. A couple more woman did the same and I accepted that I had found my first topless beach.

After an hour or so of relaxing on the sand, jotting in my notebook, I decided it was time to get high. On the walking tour my guide told us of a castle not too far from the city center called Montjuïc Castle which offered great views of the city. It was a bit of a walk but I didn't mind. At that point in the journey I was used to walking for ten hours a day plus the architecture of Barcelona offered so many interesting sightseeing opportunities. I walked along the boardwalk past smiling faces and rollerbladers, through the streets passing musicians of varying genres and skill, walked through an anarchists bookstore with an old man reading about Che behind the counter, and found myself walking the perimeter of Montjuïc Castle overlooking the city center on one side and the ocean on the other.

From the castle walls I noticed a building resembling a kind of arena and decided to explore. The path down from the castle was beautiful, wandering through trees native to the arid area, cacti of which I had never seen, an outdoor restaurant with people laughing and music playing, and finally the entrance to the stadium I had seen from up high which turned out to be the Estadi Olímpic, the sight of the 1992 Summer Olympic Games. Without any kind of security or tolls to be seen I walked underneath the Olympic rings and stood at the top of the large stadium. It felt similar to the winter Olympics stadium in Norway, grand and empty, a sign of a bygone event.

After the Olympic stadium I blindly followed trails and paths hoping they would lead me back to the downtown area I had grown accustomed. Instead, I emerged from the trees with an elegant building in front of me, the Museu Nacional D'Art de Catalunya. Walking around the edge of the grand building the view opened itself and as I stood in front of the museum my mouth dropped. Below me was a magnificent kind of pedestrian drive which led down to a stadium surrounded by bustling people and vehicles. Ornate fountains and Greek-inspired white columns gave way to a busy road splitting through Venice-inspired red bricked pillars, and ending with a large fountain in the middle of a traffic circle. Barcelona couldn't help but astound with beauty.

The following day I started out with the intention of exploring the city by chasing the architecture of the famed Catalonian designer Antoni Gaudí. During the walking tour on my first day in the city our guide praised the modernist design work of the architect who I had never heard of before. I looked into taking a guided tour but it was quite expensive and since Gaudí designed the buildings to be beautiful on the inside as well as outside I figured I could do it myself. Armed with a map circled with many different locations I set out in the cloudy morning in search of beauty and art, two things Barcelona had covered.

Trekking back to the area surrounding the Arc de Triomf, I began my Gaudí tour with the Cascada Fountain. As the name implies it is a fountain surrounded by palm trees ornamented with a gold chariot on top, beautiful white marble as its body, and a large fountain at the base. The area surrounding it was full of people enjoying life and basking in the sun which had begun peaking out from behind the grey clouds. Next was Gaudí's most famous work La Sagrada Família, the seemingly melting behemoth which has been under constant construction since the late 19th century. It wasn't hard to understand why it was his most famous work. The details were exquisite with its sharp depictions of religious scenes, honeycombed towers stretching toward the sky, and too many intricate additions which could take many days to analyze. It is truly a living work of art, grand in its ambition and large in stature.

After ducking into a small restaurant with tapas and a cold beer I ventured on through the city ticking off buildings. Along La Rambla the Palau Güell was topped with multi-colored spirals, Casa Calvet had a relatively toned-down, conventional facade, Casa Batlló with its patios resembling masks and a facade with waves and columns, and La Pedrera standing wavy, topped with snow cone shaped structures on its roof and intricate ironwork for its balconies. Walking through the streets to each of those pieces of art showed how seriously the city takes its aesthetic. Art was everywhere, the windows, on top of buildings, even the people of the city living their daily lives had a different feel to them.

The final stop on my personal Gaudi tour was Parc Güell. As the other sights were more individual works the Parc Güell was a complex of beauty. Brightly colored mosaics adorned structures which seemed straight from the mind of someone who saw the world differently. Palm trees, columns, dug out hallways with intricate designs, it was incredible. In awe of what was surrounding me I ventured out of the main complex and down a path leading to a rock formation with a large cross on its top. People were strewn all over the mound but I made my way to the top and was rewarded with a panoramic view of the city. It was an incredible end to the Gaudi tour which I couldn't have been more pleased with.

Descending from the Parc Güell I walked through the old town district once more, past the medieval walls, past the grand cathedrals, walked along the waterway with the street lights glowing, stood gazing at La Segrada Familia for the last time, and caught a movie at the English cinema. I spent the night in the hostel kitchen talking with a couple of my roommates, girls from Canada and California, and looking through the photos I had taken. There were many. Barcelona has so much to offer and I only experienced three days, three years wouldn't have been enough time. The city was so full of life and beauty, simply walking from one street to the next elevated my mood and inspired me to do more. I was falling in love with Spain and my grasp of its native tongue was getting more robust. The country seemed to beckon adventure.

The bus rocked its way down the arid land heading toward the middle of Spain. We picked up passengers in the large city of Zaragoza and at 1:30 stopped in the middle of nowhere for lunch. The only building within sight was a market with a small gas station attached. The bus' inhabitants climbed off looking tired, we grabbed sandwiches and snacks then back on the bus. Another two hours and we were at the edge of Madrid in a large bus depot far from the city center and my hostel. With a sigh, like so many sighs before, I started walking.

    Travel days were always a mixed bag of feelings. Just when I was getting comfortable with the previous city I packed up my things, said my goodbyes to the acquaintances I had made, and ventured off into the unknown to do the same thing over again. It was equal parts exhilarating as it was nerve racking, but it was a kind of existence which forced me to live in the moment every day. The two hour walk to the central section of Madrid gave me plenty of time to process all of those emotions, once amid the tourists I ducked into a taco restaurant to recharge.

As I was eating, a young couple came up to me and asked if I was a backpacker, I told them I was, and we began talking about the lifestyle, the things I had seen, and what lay ahead. They both were surprised at how quickly I was going through countries and vowed they would do a similar venture in the near future. We laughed and parted ways.

The first hours in a city the size of Madrid are always a whirlwind. Everything is in your face, fast paced and grand, plus there is no guarantee of a peaceful home base so there is a tension. Up until then I had stayed in more sub-par hostels than great ones so I kept my expectations quite low but once I walked into the hostel I was to be staying all my anxiety quickly vanished. Unlike the hostel in Barcelona, the front desk attendants were extremely nice, the bar was in the lobby with bright lights and clean with young people all around talking, playing a guitar, and laughing. It felt warm and I was pleased.

I found my room which was empty, took a fast shower then headed down for a drink. After a beer the bartender offered me a Tinto. I had never heard of it, she was appalled and poured me one. Tinto, it turned out, is a carbonated beverage made of red wine and soda served on draft and is quite popular in Spain. I drank long from the cold, fizzy drink and was hooked, it was delicious. After a two Tinto's I decided to call it quits for the evening and go back to my room for an early night. I was surprised to find a woman on the opposing bunk typing away, smiling at me as I entered.

The woman was French, 36 years old, and a journalist, an inexperienced one who was new to her work. We instantly connected and talked non-stop about writing, books, journalism, and our home countries. I asked her why she was in Madrid and she explained she had been asked to write a story about a holy man, a kind of guru, residing in the desert outside Madrid. I was instantly intrigued and asked for more information. In her broken English and thick French accent she told me the story of how she had been working on the story for a few days, venturing out into the desert, meeting with the guru and his disciples, recording statements, then transcribing it all. We walked out onto our room's patio and both leaned against the cool wrought iron bars in the warm evening as she continued her story.

"The guru and his people are not the ones who have been most strange for me. On the way back to the city this afternoon I was standing there minding my own business when an old man, probably 80 years old, walked up to me and grabbed my breast! I was shocked. Before I could say anything the women around me stood up quickly and used their purses to hit him and the bus driver stopped and the old man shuffled off." The French woman said this with a smirk on her face not looking as offended as I thought she should have been.

"That is crazy! What happened after that?" I said, not believing what I was hearing.

"The bus driver asked if I was okay and I said 'yes' and the women told me he was an old pervert with mental problems that grabs women all the time."

"That's not okay," I said. "Why don't they do something about him?"

"And what would that do? He is not right in the head, it would be cruel to lock him way for that."

The conversation shifted to other topics and before long we said our good nights and went to bed. I laid awake that night thinking about the French journalist sleeping mere feet away from me and wishing her the best. Something about the way she told the story and reacted to being assaulted didn't sit well with me. The next morning I woke up, rolled over and noticed the bed which she had occupied was empty and the sheets were pristinely folded. What an interesting person.

Through the hostel, I booked a walking tour of the city which introduced me to other travelers who shared interests similar to mine and showed us the major sights. Our group walked through medieval squares, passed fortresses and elaborate cathedrals, and ended in a district full of shops and places to eat. A group of six of us got together and had traditional Spanish churros we dipped in melted chocolate.

Back at the hostel three guys and myself walked to an inner city park (Parque de El Retiro) and saw the Fountain of the Fallen Angel, a black stone portrayal of Lucifer, and walked to the main bullfighting ring of Madrid. After having spent all day exploring the city together we raised glasses over a three course meal the hostel was putting on. The drinks were included with the meal so the twelve of us slammed drinks and ate, laughing and talking.

We retired to our rooms to change then met back in the lobby, tonight was to be my first hostel-led pub crawl. Looking back, I'm not sure why I hadn't partaken in the numerous pub crawls I had been offered before Madrid. That hostel was different. I felt like I had made real connections with the other travelers and felt like I would have fun.

Our pub crawl leader was a young twitchy Spaniard named Carlos. Loud and suave he corralled the twelve of us together, which was a bit of a challenge since we had already been drinking, and we walked to the first bar. There were to be a total of four bars included in the package, a set amount of time at each, and a shot of tequila available upon entry into each establishment.

The first bar was a club with strobe lights, expensive drinks, and people grinding on each other. Our group took the tequila shot and I drank about three sangrias. The second bar had a line to get in and a few of the girls from our group had water thrown on them from residents in the flat above the bar. Designed in more of a labyrinth, this bar seemed sketchy and had way too expensive of drinks. Standing in the corner I talked to some people including an American guy, who just got back from Tel Aviv, about Jack Kerouac and writing for a bit. By the time the third bar rolled around I was feeling buzzed and not enjoying the club experience, I never have, and told Carlos, our leader, I was going to head back to the hostel. Acting offended and a bit worried he offered me some weed and told me he would pay for my drinks but I told him "no." I think he thought I was more drunk than I actually was and started pushing me towards the entrance, I ducked my shoulder and walked away from him not liking the vibe.

It was probably about three in the morning as I walked back to my hostel, just drunk enough to enjoy the smells of the air and the coolness of the night but not too far gone to have the spins. Back at the hostel the lobby lights were dim, I pulled out my notebook and sat at the empty bar to jot down some notes. A good looking woman walked behind the bar and asked if I wanted a drink. I had a Tinto and we spoke for a bit, not about travel but normal things, mundane things.

She apologized for the way the pub crawl leader acted and bought me another drink. Out of nowhere a young girl from New York came up to me and asked if I wanted to watch a movie in the basement. I followed her down into the laundry area of the hostel where a few other late-night travelers were drinking and watching a movie, the conversation was incredible, the people so diverse. Before long others from the pub crawl came in drunk with more booze.

I finally called it quits around five, stumbled up to my empty room and passed out. For some unknown reason I woke up three hours later feeling refreshed and ventured down to have a much needed breakfast. One of the guys I had taken the walking tour with and drank alongside at the pub crawl was already down eating with bloodshot eyes. We swapped stories from the night before and he asked me to go with him to Toledo, about an hour from Madrid, in a few minutes. Without a thought to how tired I was or the amount of alcohol I had consumed I agreed. We both downed our black coffees and boarded the shuttle van to Toledo.

The van settled on a hill overlooking the medieval city of Toledo with its Cathedrals and square fortress looming large over the red roofs. Surrounding the city was the same arid land of central Spain I had grown accustomed to which made the blue river, the Tagus, winding around the city that much more stark. We all took panoramic photos and were driven down to the entrance of Toledo next to the large fortress. Luke, the late thirties Nova Scotian I had met on the walking tour and partied with the night before, and I had met a nineteen year old Irish guy named Zak on the way over. The three of us clicked and we decided to explore together.

It wasn't since Reed left back in Denmark had I truly explored with anyone else. Along the way there had been a few fair-weather travelers I associated with but Luke and Zak had the same interests as I did plus they were relaxed and easy going, two great qualities in travel companions. We walked along the cobble stoned streets under the flags of the ancients, past a couple grand cathedrals and walked in one, and ultimately ventured to the edges of the old town walls. It was a beautiful city but after a couple of hours the events of the previous night began to take its hold on our energy levels so we did what any good traveler does in a time of need, found a bar.

Over pizza and beer tucked away in a cobble stoned alley the three of us talked about all manner of things. Loves had and loves lost, travel, home life, work and school, and in the end left the restaurant with each of us ensuring we would have a place to stay in the Pacific Northwest, Nova Scotia, and the coasts of Ireland. After another zigzag across Toledo we found our shuttle and travelled back to Madrid.

It was nearing dusk so the three of us found a small bar serving tapas on the bustling streets near the central district and heard one of the art museums, Reina Sofía, was dropping their entrance fee for the evening. The beers went down smooth and we stood in line to get in the grand museum with hundreds of others, talking to those in the line like it was an extension of our hostel. Once in we grabbed a map and took off in all directions.

The Reina Sofía was the first large art museum I had partaken in through the entirety of my drifting through Europe and I was not let down. Filled with all mediums and movements of Spanish art, the museum was large and well layered. We saw some of my favorite artists Man Ray, Dalí, and early work from Picasso. As we continued through work after work the Picasso area seemed to have a large congregation of people, after more investigation it was due to the *Guernica*, his mesmerizing painting while in his blue period.

We must have spent three hours in the museum before we walked out into the warm Spanish night. Back to the hostel we went looking forward to our trip the following day to a different city. Luke and I dropped Zak off at his hostel, not far from ours, stopped in to a great restaurant for kebabs, then back to our hostel for a Tinto. After being awake for 21 hours I was zonked and made my way to my room. It was empty and my imagination ran off with thoughts of my French roommate and her guru in the deserts of Spain.

In the same way as the previous day, I woke and went down to the lobby to find Luke hunched over a bowl of oatmeal with black coffee steaming. It turned out he had gone to the clubs after leaving me and had stayed up even later than before. Unfortunately for him our tickets were already purchased, we met Zak in the train station, boarded a bus, and were off to Segovia.

With cloudless blue skies guiding our exploration we bounded through the ancient streets of Segovia with its earth toned buildings until we found a castle, Alcázar de Segovia, fit for a fantasy. Perched on the edge of the city looking out to the arid countryside outside the city walls was the huge, blocky, gothic turreted castle. After a moment to comprehend how fitting the castle was within those ancient city walls we paid the fee and entered. I had never been *inside* a proper castle's innards before and it was everything I had ever dreamed.

Once inside the castle a courtyard opened up revealing a square of rooms some with swords hanging in a cross on the walls with suits of armor and shields, others housed gigantic wooden dining tables with goblets and animal skins on the wall. We climbed to the top of Johns Tower ascending the tight, narrow-stepped staircase until we were looking over the city and countryside. The three of us walked along every cobble of that castle taking in as much as we could. While on top of the tower we used our map to circle where we wanted to venture next.

Bigger than it seemed, Segovia had many alleys and squares not outright visible even from as high a point as the castle's tower. Cathedrals were magnificent, people cruising across their squares laughing and enjoying the blue skies. After crossing most of the map's sights off we came to the Roman aqueducts and were caught off guard. Towering at 100 feet tall at its highest point, the aqueducts were composed of giant grey stones assembled with the greatest technology the time had to offer. Climbing to a point equal to the tops of the aqueducts we stood admiring the structure as it ran along the city reflecting within residential windows and being admired by a diverse array of people.

Luke, Zak, and I separated a bit and spent some time reflecting on what we were seeing. I was grateful to have the two of them to talk about what I was seeing, to have someone to bounce ideas off and get different opinions on things I had never seen before and which arose questions never posed in my head. We took our time getting back to the bus station, basking in the beauty all around us and knowing once we returned to Madrid we would be parting ways with a high probability of never seeing each other again. In some ways it was sad but in others, it gave a kind of beauty to the short friendships which have no choice to be sudden, bright, and ultimately die out as quickly as they began.

The hostel bar that last night in Madrid was a chaotic mess in the best possible way. As the universe sometimes does, timing was coincidental and most of the people I had made friends with were all leaving on other journeys. We toasted to the clubs and the sights we had seen, we toasted to the journeys which had guided us all to that wonderful hostel in Madrid and smiled with twinkles in our eyes at what lay ahead for each of us. The Tinto was pouring into late that evening, we all said our goodbyes, and walked off into our rooms.

The bus arrived to Pamplona around six in the evening and, as usual, I had no idea where I was going. In great contrast to the cities I had been in, Pamplona was much more relaxed, even tranquil in the warm evening air. Before long I arrived to my hostel, was shown around, offered to have laundry done, walked out onto the terrace overlooking a quiet street, and was back out the door.

In almost all of the previous cities I arrived with little to no planning and relied on getting lost to show me the way. Pamplona was different due to one name; Ernest Hemingway. The entire reason Pamplona was on the map was because of the famed writer and his first novel *The Sun Also Rises*, written in 1926 when Hemingway was 27 years old. The book revolves around a group of young people who travel to the city for the San Fermin festival and indulge in bullfighting, and ultimately come to realize the flaws of their way of life. Because of that book, Pamplona was like a kind of literary pilgrimage but first I needed to buy the book.

Within a few short minutes of walking I found myself in the middle of the Plaza del Castillo, the main square of the old town district lined on all four corners with hotels and other buildings looking like they hadn't changed since the twenties. There I found a bookstore, I hunted down a copy of the book, found a dingy bar, ordered a tall beer, and sat in the corner reading *Fiesta: The Sun Also Rises* (in Spain the title has "Fiesta" added to it). After a couple beers and a few dozen pages read I walked around the old town for a bit enjoying the buzz from the beer and how it enhanced the warm nights air and found my way back to the hostel.

One of the hostel's workers was a guy about my age with a messy beard, thick rimmed glasses, and a laid back vibe who I instantly began speaking to. We exchanged the usual pleasantries of hostel life but soon transitioned into writing. The two of us talked for some time out on the terrace about writers, writing styles, and what kind of books we wanted to write in the future. The hours slipped by and we made our way into the common room to find three Danish guys, and two girls staring at the television with big eyes and open mouths.

It was November 13, 2015 and that night in Paris terrorists killed over 130 people. We all gazed stupidly at the images on the screen, the bodies being wheeled out on stretchers, sounds of gun shots, and words running across the screen in Spanish. The guys from Denmark were just beginning the Camino de Santiago and the two girls just arrived from France and my next stop was the south of France. Between the long, silent stares at the television we talked quickly about how sorry we felt for those who lost their lives and speculated at how it would affect our individual movement through the European Union. We talked until three that morning about our loved ones back home and how evil in the world can rear its mutilated head in the most nonsensical ways.

The next morning I went back to sitting in front of the same television screen looking up the state of the countries within the EU. France had declared a kind of border freeze and I heard through different sources they were not allowing anyone to enter or leave France for the next day or two. Selfishly I was worried because France was my next stop, I was to be in Toulouse the following day. Worried, I went down to the bus station and bought a ticket which they sold me. I was surprised but tucked the ticket in my pack, wondering if they would void it the next day.

Trying to take my mind off the terrorist attacks only hours away, I walked to the square from the night before and ate at the Care Iruña. Its black and white checkered tile floors and vintage decor couldn't have been much different than how the restaurant looked back in the twenties when Hemingway and his friends drank too much just outside. I spent the day tracing the path of the Running of Bulls, walking from the starting stables to the bullring not too far away, stood outside the beautiful churches which seemed too big for a town of that size, walked around La Ciudadela with its 16th century walls in the shape of a pentagon, and people watched at the town hall, Ayuntamiento, with its colorful flags with wooden fences around it to keep the bulls from straying off their path to slaughter.

I wandered all over that wondrous town. It felt as if I was living there, walking here and there with a book under one arm, ducking into small shops and cafes, drinking with the locals at bars, reading my book amidst wandering tourists. The city was welcoming and warm, a place where a traveler feels like they can assimilate and belong.

Those two and a half days in Pamplona seemed to go so fast. The final morning I walked once more across the large square, ate breakfast at the Cafe Iruña, and made my way to the bus depot nervously waiting to see if they would accept my ticket into France amid the violence and uncertainty which had cast a shadow over a country known for its bright lights.

Without ceremony, the bus driver glanced quickly at my passport, took my ticket, and I sat down on the nice coach bound for Toulouse. With headphones in and my shoulder bouncing gently against the window we passed the imaginary line between Spain and France, no one gave us a second look as we travelled north. In a few days I would be in Paris, the French countryside put me at ease.

Chapter 15

France

The southern terminus of France is beautiful. As our bus wound through the countryside my earbuds were blasting country western music and my long hair bounced upon my shoulders. The bus was not crowded and not too long into our journey north a young guy in the seat in front of me turned and asked what I was listening to. Taking my earbuds out, I told him which sparked a big debate in music, how country western music was nothing but shit, and how metal was the best. We didn't stop talking the remainder of the way to Toulouse.

The young guy was about 22 years old and Canadian with a peach fuzz mustache and earnest eyes which seemed to be intelligent and kind. Our bus arrived in the relatively small city of Toulouse around 9:00 in the evening and it turned out the Canadian and I were booked at the same hostel. After some small talk with the proprietor of the hostel we were shown our room, a large square with four sets of bunkbeds lining each wall. Eager to stretch our legs we set out on a walk through town.

In our topic weaving discussion on the bus ride it came up we each had a burgeoning fascination with photography. We spent our first night wandering down to the river showing each other the little we knew about ISO and f-stop and how to take a half-way decent picture at night. After awhile of walking we came to a large open square and saw a candle-light vigil being held for those lost in the Paris attacks. It was around midnight but the vigil supported a couple dozen people, some in tears others drawing French phrases on the ground, everyone was somber.

As I gazed at the candles and the handmade signs plastered to the building I couldn't help but feel a grief which I had never experienced. All of the problems of the world seem so far away to my isolationist country, even the attack on the World Trade Centers was over 3000 miles away, from home in rural Oregon, but there, in France, the attacks were all too close which made them real. My Canadian comrade had tears in his eyes most of the way back to the hostel. There wasn't much to discuss.

The morning was a bit dreary as I made my way to a quaint corner bakery and had a croissant. My Canadian friend and I decided we enjoyed each others company enough to explore more of the city together so we set off toward the river. We must have looked like proper tourists with our cameras around our necks stopping every few minutes to capture a purple window shutter or the light fixtures adorning the side of a building.

After hours of walking the cobble stoned roads we wanted to find a high spot to see the city from above. Not wanting to spend any money we talked to the right people who told us to go to the top of a department store in the shopping district downtown. Dubious of the advice, we walked in the front doors of the large store, walked past the cosmetics with their heavily perfumed air, and took the elevator to the top.

Stepping out onto the terrace of the building proved our intuitions wrong. The city sprawled out before us with its red roofs and typical French chimneys. We took our photos and marveled at our luck. After an hour of walking back and forth, smiling with astonishment we descended the building and left through the perfumed air ready for more adventure. Where better for that than a bar?

The Canadian and I had our first beer at a pizza restaurant around six. We met some interesting people and the wood fired pizza was amazing. The next bar was dull but the beer was cold. The third bar was close to the river and looked like a kind of sports bar from the outside. We decided to give it a shot and entered to find the walls were littered with polaroids of women lifting up their tops to expose their bare breasts. Smiling at the incredible number of photos, we went to the bar, received our beers in plastic cups, and migrated to the back area which housed a foosball table.

We started playing the game haphazardly as a way to pass the time between sips of beer. Within minutes of playing, two young French guys came over and asked if we wanted to make a bet? Not thinking anything of it we obliged agreeing to play against the two, losers buy beers for the others. Within seconds we knew we had made a mistake. I have never before seen anyone as good at a table game as those two Frenchmen were. It was ridiculous the level of skill they possessed in manipulating those little men and the speed that soccer ball had as it found our goal ten times before we could even score one. Realizing we had been hustled, we bought the Frenchmen beers and vowed to not play more foosball.

Feeling bad for the trick they had played, the Frenchmen offered to buy us a shot, we accepted. The bartender and the Frenchmen were all good friends and were shocked we had never been to France let alone Toulouse let alone their favorite bar in all the world. The five of us began telling stories and drinking heavily. Each shot was apparently the epitome of French cuisine, if one was to believe the bartender, and they kept passing them our way. After maybe six shots in, a few more younger French guys walked in and they also knew the bartender and the two guys who had hustled us. Instantly we became friends and more shots were had.

The other guys were getting tired of there being no women in the bar so they asked if we wanted to go to a *real* French bar. Quite drunk, my Canadian friend and I yelled in acceptance but first we had to take the last shot. With a wink to the bartender, all of the Frenchmen smiled and began telling us some bullshit origin story behind the alcohol they called "The Antichrist." From deep below the bar a tall bottle with a cracked cork was brought out containing red liquid with chunks floating. The mood in the bar shifted from one of joviality to seriousness as the bartender poured all of us, including himself, a shot from the demonic elixir.

Like some sort of ancestral toast we lifted our glasses in the air and threw back the red liquid, it burned its way down our throats and landed with a thud in our stomachs. We all cheered and wiped our lips, some quivering from the disgusting taste. Without hesitation we exited the bar with the topless girls on the walls and migrated not too far away to a packed yellow painted bar.

The bar was out of control. It was like a mix between a college party and a punk rock concert. Every inch of the building was covered with sweaty young people dancing and grinding to loud French music, plastic cups sloshing out the myriad liquids which lie within. Our small group bellied up to the bar and a shot was quickly thrown back then a plastic cup of beer took its place. By now my head was spinning with the sheer volume of alcohol I had consumed not to mention the variety of foreign swill sloshing in my gut. A few more people joined our group including one man who looked much older than the rest of us with his closely cropped hair and denim jacket. Hearing we were from North America this new guy left and returned with shot glasses for each of our group which he quickly lit ablaze. The shot went down smoother than I thought but the room started to spin.

I looked at my Canadian comrade and his eyes told me he was in the same headspace. The rest of our group was sad we were leaving and amidst the loud music and dancing people all around we hugged one another, exchanged contact information, and said our goodbyes. The air was cool as we stumbled out the door from the yellow bar not entirely sure how to get back to our hostel. Loudly we exclaimed how grateful we were to have all of our shots bought, every one, for us that night and what an amazing country France was!

Our room was completely quiet as we walked in but soon realized a head was poking out of one of the bunks which wasn't there when we left. Trying to be quiet, an objective I'm only too sure we failed, we found our bunks and laid our drunken heads. I couldn't come close to estimating how many drinks I had had that night, it was truly too many to count.

The bus pulled up behind the main train station in Lyon around dusk and people were everywhere. This is to be expected from a train depot in one of the larger cities in France but after hours of riding on a bus the last thing I wanted to do was navigate through commuters trying to get home or to a party or to wherever they were trying to go that Friday night. Like so many times before, I gathered my small backpack and began to weave through the bustle of the station to make it to the other side. I had found the first hour or so in a new city to be such a stressful time. Nothing is familiar, the faces all seem to be looking at you and all my mind turned to a tunnel-visioned mess of "got to get to the hostel!"

After weaving through the downtown shopping center and being harassed by two homeless Frenchmen trying to sell me stolen watches, I walked across a bridge and watched the beautiful purple sunset over some large buildings. It was now officially dark and the masses of people just kept sliding past me. Eventually I made my way through a restaurant-lined alley with tables on the streets and young, hip people in chairs drinking wine and food I couldn't afford. Turning a corner I passed a McDonald's advertising Big Macs for 12 euro and shook my head with anxiety and hunger.

At the end of the block my GPS said I had found my hostel but there was no street name nor building number to be found, just an abnormally large wooden door and a keypad to the right of it. Remembering the confirmation email, I pulled up the directions on how to get in. Pushing the corresponding numbers an apathetic voice came over the speaker and asked something in French. Guessing, I responded with "I have a reservation to stay for the night," to which the voice responded with a "oui" and a loud buzz clicked the door and I walked in.

Passing through the long dark walkway I noticed mailboxes and a sign above notifying me that my hostel was on the fourth floor. The automatic lights weren't doing their job and I ascended the stone stairs in partial darkness with only the faint voices of people above to assure me I was heading in the right direction. Once I reached the fourth floor two guys my age were sitting on a window ledge smoking weed and nodded their head up as I passed them and pushed the door with HOSTEL gleaming white above.

The floor plan was strange for a hostel, it seemed to have been a large apartment at one time with three rooms to the left and five to the right of the entrance. Young people were walking around looking at me with hints of curiosity but no one said anything even though I could have been anyone. Hesitantly I walked to the first room on the right and everyone looked up at once while the music continued to play loudly from a surround sound set up with speakers in all four corners.

The room looked like a college dorm with a huge map of the world hanging next to posters of Bob Dylan and Jim Morrison. A black couch was below the map with three people in their mid-twenties drinking wine and smiling and speaking French. Next to the window overlooking downtown Lyon was an older guy, maybe 35 years old, who I could tell was American before he ever spoke a word, he was one of those guys who exuded the typical American vibe. Looking to the left was a black bookcase which covered the entire wall and was filled with used paperbacks in various forms of abuse, some in French some in English all in disarray. In the corner where the bookcase wall met the window wall was a handsome blonde guy, again in his mid-twenties, behind a desk. The guy leaned back in his leather chair and instantly asked "where in America are you from?"

Taken aback by his spot on question I responded, "I'm from Oregon, I have a reservation to stay here for two nights." A girl sitting in a black leather armchair directly in front of the desk stood up slowly and with an accent said "welcome" as she smiled and passed with a glass of red wine in her hand.

"Welcome mate. You're just in time for happy hour, are you feelin' some wine?" One of the guys on the couch below the world map asked motioning toward a half empty bottle of Bordeaux on the blonde guy's desk. Looking back

I'm fairly sure the guy was English by his accent but he looked Indian especially with his shoulder length black hair and Lenny Kravitz way of holding himself.

"Sure," was all I could respond with and sat in the chair in front of the desk and poured myself a glass full of wine.

It was then the blonde guy introduced himself and took my passport and did the typical checking-in process. The room was so full of life all I could do was look around and try to keep up. The American next to the window kept talking about California while the three on the couch were telling him how France was the place to be. People would walk into the room with more wine bottles and begin talking like they had been staying in the hostel for weeks. With the music blaring and the people talking it was all I could do to catch the words the reception worker was saying. After a few minutes of feeling like a complete outsider the guy took me to my room for the night, a ten bed dorm with white bunks and mattresses with stains.

I chose the bunk closest to the door and began putting linens over the stains on the bottom mattress. A younger girl was reading on the bottom bunk on the opposite side of the room and we began talking about our travels. After a while another girl walked into the room. This girl was bubbly and loud and was not shy to run over and shake my hand and tell me how happy she was to meet another American and ask me where I was from and tell me she was from California.

We all spoke quickly like all people in hostels do, telling each other where we've been and where we were heading. A hostel is an amazing environment unlike any other for conversation. Once you open the door there are people from all over the world waiting inside, ready to talk about all manner of things. Everyone is giddy and excited about what they are doing and where they have been and want to know where you've been because maybe you know something they don't. Majority of the people in a hostel are between 18 and 35 so we all have similar interests and ways of looking at the world but our backgrounds are all different and the conversations fly and the words are rapid and once one more person opens that door the stories start over but no one is upset to tell the same stories because we are all travelers and doing something unique.

Once the stories began to fade I asked the girls if "there was a grocery store nearby" and they said "yes" and I went out into the French night. Passing a bakery with a red awning closed for the night and a burger place with people outside I found the market and bought a quick dinner of sandwich and chips and, of course, cheap French wine.

Back at the hostel I found the kitchen and it was packed with three guys from Greece hitting on a girl from New York to little gain. Finding a bottle opener I stood against the counter listening to the foreign pick-up lines while opening the bottle. People are the same all over. After my meager dinner I brought the bottle of wine back to my room and began writing in my little journal.

There was constant commotion around the hostel halls. Various languages would be screamed at all times of night with music coming from all the rooms with different genres and languages clashing into a cacophony of cultural bliss. The beds in my room began to fill up with a thirty year old from Sweden across from me plucking on a ukulele and an American to my right with a book on neuroscience. The Swedish guy found out I had been to Sweden and began asking me all sorts of questions.

Did I like it, where was my favorite place, had I gone to any metal concerts? The entire time we talked he was fiddling with his ukulele and I realized he was playing it with the most skill I had ever heard anyone play the quirky little instrument. Eventually I asked him where he got it and he responded he just bought it maybe a week ago. "I teach classical guitar back in Sweden," he said, "but didn't want to bring a full sized guitar with me on the trip so I found this little guy last week in Germany. Really I've just been plucking at it trying to make it sound half-way decent."

The Swede was about six foot five with blonde hair and blonde beard. The way he spoke was gentle and his English was amazing, as is the case with the majority of Scandinavians. The whole room responded with compliments about the playing, compliments the Swede modestly accepted.

After the conversation began to sway away from me I turned to the guy to my right with the neuroscience book in his hands and soon got lost in conversation with him. It turned out he had just completed his undergraduate and was at a cross roads between graduate school and travel, much like I found myself at the time. The focus he had been leaning towards was more clinical while my focus had been consciousness, a field which I had done the bulk of my neuroscience research while completing my undergraduate.

Once we each established our backgrounds the philosophy began to fly. First delving into the nuances of consciousness we quickly followed up on the temporality of EEG and the lack of such in fMRI with understanding real-time studies. Within minutes our brains were clicking on all cylinders and the subject of statistics flooded the space between us. Commenting on multivariate ANOVA and chi-squares and how we each had wanted to do meta-analysis research of our own topics, mine in evolutionary psychology and his in drug effects. The conversation reached a crescendo and we each became silent. I hadn't had that kind of talk for some time and it felt good to squeeze my brain like that in a hostel in France, a place I had no intention of ever bringing up that kind of science. Everyone in the room looked towards us with strange looks and the giddy girl in the corner commented "that was really interesting."

The room became mostly quiet after the explosion everyone had just had amongst their cliques. I had continued to drink my wine with headphones blasting music into my ears and journal getting frantically scribbled upon. Around midnight our Swedish friend began to play his ukulele only this time louder which seemed to carry the sound around the hostel and brought the long haired Indian guy I had met in the reception room in with a backpacker guitar. "Hoy mate, you mind if we jam together?"

The Swede smiled with confirmation and the two of them began to harmonize with the two instruments. It didn't take long for a younger guy with bright red hair and a full sized guitar to walk in and join the sound making while one of the girls sat in the mix and began singing. Within no time the four of them began covering songs and got louder, loud enough where people I hadn't seen in the hostel before came to our door frame to lean and listen to the jam session.

So there we were, a room full of strangers playing beautiful music and talking about neuroscience and travels around the world all the while drinking wine and looking out at the cool night spreading over Lyon in a hostel full of young people on a Friday night. All of us the same in the way we wanted to live that night, together and conversing about things we didn't know and things we did and sharing stories of what we have done and will do. In the background were the high pitched laughs of the Greeks yelling stories and the smell of marijuana wafting here and there. The hostel with only two bathrooms for so many people and a kitchen with so many empty wine bottles but no one making food. All of us stayed up late listening to music and telling stories and feeling the most present, for moments like that are truly such. Rejoicing in our youth and living in that moment despite the atrocity which happened to Paris less than a week before.

When I think of that hostel I think of a bohemian life and that life is one I wish to live for some time to come because that life is a good life, at least for the ones who accept it as such. To live a unique life, a life untethered by social norms and one in the pursuit of understanding and wanting to know more of things we know less; that is the bohemian lifestyle of today and that lifestyle is the one I experienced in that hostel and, at least for those two nights, there was no place I'd rather have been.

It was raining on my way to Paris. The bus pounded on down the freeway as I was lost in conversation with an alternative girl, from Paris originally, and her Canadian boyfriend. They were on their way to see her family and were both excited to spend time in the city of lights, the same city on so many postcards, the same city which people actually lived and worked and went about their normal days. Excitement flooded my body as the upper portions of the Eiffel Tower stuck out from behind the plain buildings lining the roadway.

Our bus parked far from the city center, as was common with my cheap travel options, and I pulled out the rickety umbrella I had picked up in Brno. With a vague understanding of where I was going I began walking down a bustling street until I was face-to-face with the Arc de Triomphe. To my confusion the iconic arc was situated in the middle of a busy roundabout, I followed signs, hurried through an underground tunnel and soon emerged on the other side looking up at the inscriptions lining the underbelly of the Arc surrounded by heavily armed police with bullet-proof vests and weary looks upon their faces. It was then the full weight of the terrorist attacks just days previous took hold and I began to selfishly worry that the care-free Paris of old would be long gone.

Leaving the Arc de Triomphe I walked down the Champs Élysées humming its familiar tune in my head, taking in the sights of upscale Paris and imagining the history which the street had seen. As usual, I ducked down side streets to get away from the swarm of tourists and tried to feel the residential vibes. By then the rain had slowed and the grey clouds amidst the buildings leant the city a gothic but inviting atmosphere.

Like any other building, the Eiffel Tower snuck into my view through the residential buildings. A flutter went through me as I began my chase. Over bridges with locks and small inscriptions, past the locals at the bistros and despite the rain I hurried until the tower stood stark in front of me. I looked up mesmerized by one of the most iconic buildings in the world. Standing there in the Champs de Mars looking up at the iron beast I felt a weight on me. Strangely the entire trip through Europe, despite all of the amazing sights I had seen, somehow culminated in standing in front of the Eiffel Tower in the sprinkling rain. The entire trip suddenly made sense. It was like a kind of magnum opus presenting its beauty to the beholder. I was over halfway through my trek around Europe but it seemed I had found the hot burning center of the trip. Everything else radiated out from it. This was its focal point.

The clouds began to darken and the rain came back. I remembered a movie which payed homage to the city of lights stating Paris is best in the rain, as I walked away from the tower amidst the cacophony of accents and couples leaning on one another under myriad umbrellas I understood what they meant. I left, crossed the Seine and stood in awe at the Louvre all lit up in the dark. Its glass pyramid a stark contrast to the gothic body of the museum behind.

My hostel was situated on the same street as the Moulin Rouge, quite a distance from the Louvre, which gave me ample opportunity to experience the city in the rain. I arrived drenched but drunk with excitement, checked into the dingy old hotel-turned-hostel, and found my room. After a quick change of clothes I hurried back out into the rain to explore the 18th Arrondissement. The streets were teeming as the red lights from the windmill-topped Moulin Rouge cast its sinful glow to the pedestrians below. After some exploration I ducked into a side market, bought cheap French wine, and found my way back to the common room of my hostel. The bottle didn't stand a chance as I planned out the next few days in the wonderful city.

The morning came suddenly as I hurried through breakfast and found myself, shoulders hunched walking through the rain on my way to the Louvre. It was early so the lines were not like all the terrible stories I had been hearing for months. Once inside my legs bounded with excitement past the throngs of tourists. With eyes devouring every painting and every statue, I combed the museum for five hours before standing at the exit a bit disappointed.

How could I be let down by one, if not *the*, best museum in the world? I had seen the Mona Lisa surrounded by immense works on all sides of her small frame. I had seen Venus de Milo, Napolean's apartments, the Winged Victory of Samothrace, the Virgin on the Rocks, and the pilfered antiquities of Egypt but felt something was missing. The rain had increased in the five hours I had spent in the grand museum and the streets seemed to have swollen immensely.

With Czech umbrella in hand I trudged along with only my burning excitement to keep me warm. Nortre-Dame stood beautifully gothic and grand, gargoyles sputtering water from all sides. Crossing the Seine I found refuge in Shakespeare and Company, a functional bookstore where prominent writers of the past, Hemingway with Joyce and Stein, spent their time thumbing through books they couldn't afford.

Upon entering the book-worm paradise I was greeted by a "feed the starving writers" sign situated in the floorboards underneath a plexiglass shield. Walking along book-heavy shelves with small nooks carved out here and there with the smell of must and thick pages wafting I was happy. The rain outside completed the atmosphere of the small establishment which had seen so many faces pass through its green doors. Before leaving I purchased Hemingway's *A Moveable Feast*, a brilliant book about his younger years spent in Paris, and made my way down the Latin Quarter of the city with the rain coming down in buckets.

Past the Sorbonne, through the Jardin du Luxembourg, up and down countless alleys and side streets I made it back to the Champs de Mars with the Eiffel Tower. Night was beginning to fall as I made a final push and walked into the entrance to the Catacombs of Paris. The ticket booth looks like an old train station booth with its heavily grouted tile floors and flickering light feel.

I descended what seemed like a mile then walked through a long corridor of smooth earthen walls until I began seeing the remains of humans who died long ago. Dwarfing the ossuary in Brno, the Catacombs of Paris hold what is left of approximately six million people, many dying from one of the plagues that ransacked the city generations ago. The ossuary in Brno was not so much creepy as it was thought provoking. The building was designed with artistic intent and the droning music encouraged an examination of mortality in the face of death. The Catacombs of Paris are different in every way. There is no music, there is no sound. The remains are piled in heaps on either side of the walkway, many green from the algal growth of decades of moisture and dripping. It is cold and damp with minimal light and blocked off corridors to discourage tourists from getting lost. As Brno offered a meditation, Paris slapped you in the face and showed us all what death truly looked like; a heap of anonymous bones spread out each hoping to decompose as quickly as possible back into the elements from which they came.

Some people were noticeably uneasy as they shuffled through pathways. I overheard many talks of death, how each person wanted to die if given the chance, and what would happen to their bodies in such an event. As I walked through looking at skulls placed looking out into the walkway I found myself trying to picture how it would look with skin on it, who would it belong to? It was cathartic in a way, knowing that so many people had been met with the inevitability of death. Something all men must do.

After over an hour in the Catacombs I scaled the black iron spiral staircase to the world of the living. Before leaving, an apathetic worker in a black leather jacket asked to look in my backpack for any bones or other souvenirs I may have tried taking with me. I was then released out into the dark streets of Paris still wet from the day of rain. The air smelled cleaner and the lights brighter. Nothing makes life seem worth living like being face-to-face with a skull red from plague and green from dampness resting forever underneath the streets of Paris.

Morning came with more rain as I walked along the Seine, past the orange trees, and into the Musée de l'Orangerie. A fraction of the size of the Louvre, the Orangerie fit my artistic taste perfectly. The first stop was the oval rooms housing Monet's water lilies. Lining the stark white walls stretched the brilliantly simplistic impressionistic canvases. I stood getting lost in them for minutes, sometimes getting so close I could see the individual brush strokes, while others stood across the room taking them in as a whole.

Descending deeper into the museum I saw Picasso, Rousseau, Matisse, Soutine, and, my favorite painter, Amedeo Modigliani. The hairs on my arms stood erect when I realized I was looking at actual Modigliani paintings, I had to read the description plates twice just to convince myself I was standing in front of the madman's amazing work. Eyes darkened, proportions stretched, and with colors painted to give the viewer a strange, intimate feeling Modigliani has fascinated me since I first heard his story. These painters of the late nineteenth, early twentieth century were my favorites. The way they lived, the way they placed their art before so much else, the time they lived, the community of artists they were constantly surrounded by, and the age of Paris which can only be described as Golden. The museum encompassed that feeling, it was stepping back into a time when Paris and the art scene it inspired were at its peak.

Crossing the Seine I ventured over into the Musée D'Orsay, the middle ground between the impressionists at the Orangerie and the old master's of the Louvre. The museum is built from an old train station which gives it such an amazing atmosphere. It uses every inch of its two story frame, divided into different periods and styles, to give the viewer an incredible experience. Walking the halls I saw my first Van Gogh in real life, passed sculptures of such varying depictions, looked through the gigantic clock out onto the city with the Eiffel Tower stark against the grey clouds, and saw so many children in awe of the beauty surrounding us all.

    One of the exhibits which particularly caught my attention was off in a corner, shrouded in red velvet curtains. It was focused on prostitutes and the way artists ignored the social prudishness of the day to create intimate, sensual portrayals of women working in the oldest profession. Walking through the exhibit, it was refreshing to see couples of all ages discuss the beauty of these sometimes explicit portraits of prostitutes engaging in various forms of sexuality. The art was exceptional and the message even better. The belle epoch was an extraordinary time to be alive in Paris, my personal favorite of that time, Toulouse-Lautrec, embodied someone who lived it to its fullest and suffered the consequences.

    It seemed the rain would not let up no matter how many hours I spent in museums. Trudging back to the Latin Quarter for a cheap bite to eat I began to feel my feet ache with pain. Shrugging it off, I found a nice Greek restaurant, watched as the rain only worsened, then trekked back to my hostel. It was a bit early but my feet were extremely itchy and sharp pains shot up randomly. Once back to my room, with roommates gone, I took off the hiking boot style footwear I stupidly deemed fit for a walk across Europe. Since I was constantly walking, my boots never got the chance to fully dry out. Consequently, my feet were going into a wet environment each morning and remained there for all but around eight hours a day.

When I took my socks off my feet were sickly white and shrunken. The radiating pain was almost unbearable as I hobbled to the shower only to be in even more agony once I stepped into the warm water. Emerging from the bathroom feeling a bit relieved I walked into the room to a putrid smell of feet. In what could be considered one of my lowest points of the trip, I ignored the awful smell of my own rotting boots and climbed into my top bunk like the vagrant I had become. I could only imagine what my roommates, which were not the homeless wanderer-type I was morphing into, but young travelers on a simple vacation, thought upon entering our room later that evening.

I opened my eyes the next morning to find sunshine peeking through the heavy curtain in the feet-stinking atmosphere I had created. With a jolt, partially out of joy and a bit from embarrassment, I hurried downstairs and out the door and was greeted by my first sunny day in Paris. The warm rays of the sun hit my face and jolted me with energy as I found a corner bakery wafting extravagant smells and treated myself to a coffee and croissant before navigating the public transportation of Paris.

Making quick work of the underground system which I had been assured would be a nightmare, I was bounding quickly to one of my top destinations the city had to offer; a cemetery.

I made my way inside the Père Lachaise cemetery, one of the most infamous pieces of ground in the world. Having downloaded a map of the layout the night before I made my way to Oscar Wilde's place of burial first. Next was Edith Piaf, then Proust, Chopin, and Amedeo Modigliani with his surprisingly humble grave. I walked in silence past tombs with broken doors, some had elegant statues placed outside them, many gravestones were the average ones every town has while others were lavish and intricate. After getting turned around a few times more than I would have liked considering I had a map, I finally found the grave I was looking for.

With a black gate placed about six feet from the actual headstone, adorned with brightly colored ribbons and beads was laid the remains of Jim Douglas Morrison, frontman of my favorite band The Doors. In the brisk November air I placed my headphones in my ears and played my favorite live version of *The End*, the seventeen minute one with the moth joke half way through. I stood there the entire seventeen minutes, alone, thinking not only of Jim, not in some super fan kind of way, but in a homage to the ideals he stood for, the life he led, and the life we all lead. As the song progressed I closed my eyes behind my blue Ray Bans and tried to remain as present as I could be. Those moments seemed to last an eternity.

Once the song was over, a couple came up to the fence and placed a colorful ribbon around the plain black bars, a glimpse of the impact one man can have on a generation, on the world.

I left the cemetery and went up to the Montmarte district of the city. Up to the Sacré Cœur which was swarmed with people overlooking the beautiful center of Paris in the sunshine. I walked along the Seine, back to Nortre-Dame, past the Eiffel Tower, and in random tangents. I flipped through used books at small wooden bookshops, bouquinistes, situated along the Seine. I walked through the Latin Quarter, past two houses Ernest Hemingway lived in while he was young, and found Gertrude Stein's house. I was sad to leave the city of lights. I was sad to leave the people, the smells, the food, the sights, all of it.

As night fell I found myself wandering, taking in the lights and how the city felt at night. I walked past the Louvre at night, not much different than my first night in the city with the rain beating down. The city was so alive, no matter what time, there was always some place to go, something to do. Grabbing a bottle of cheap red French wine I sat in the common room of my hostel and booked my ferry ticket from the tip of Denmark to the eastern side of Iceland which would leave in less than three weeks. As the bitter red wine found its way down my throat I stared at the confirmation ticket on my tablet, there was less than three weeks left in my trip and I still had so much to see.

Like many nights before, the bottle of cheap wine was emptied and the stiff bunk bed was a welcome relief from the night. The next morning I would leave Paris, leave France, and leave the focal point of my trip not in temporality but in mind.

Chapter 16

BeNeLux

The train from Paris wound through a drizzling rain up through the French countryside, stopping for a moment in Nancy, then barreled still further north until we crossed the border of Luxembourg. Departing into the open square in front of the train station, the cold evening air hit with a northern ferocity which I hadn't experienced since standing atop an Austrian Alp weeks earlier. Each day grew closer to winter and I was only going to keep inching nearer to Iceland in the days ahead.

Pulling my scarf closer to my neck I trudged along over the open square and into the darkness of a new city. Within minutes I found myself crossing an expansive arch bridge overlooking lights far below. Never much of a fan of heights, I focused my eyes to the far end of the bridge and walked even faster than I already had been. After what felt like an hour I noticed I was on yet another bridge only this one seemed medieval. The map on my phone assured me I was nearing my hostel as I took in the pristine smelling air and clean stones and buttresses which surrounded me. With a turn I was winding down what felt like a park trail, a place a tourist fresh in a new city tries to avoid, and through trees, nestled between an expansive garden and towering arch bridge were the lights of my hostel.

As with so many times before, my heart flittered with joy and relief at having found my place of residence for the next couple days. I always envisioned the hostel acting as the allusive "X" on the map of the city; all the treasures scattered about were fine but the real treasure lie in the small, dingy bed where I would lie my head.

The hostel was quite nice and before long I was sitting in the common room with a cold pilsner in my hand and a three course Luxembourgish meal in front of me. Fellow tourists, mostly men with German sounding accents, chattered all around me while a soccer (see fútbol) game played quietly in a corner. There was talk of snow the next day as I curled into my crisp, clean sheets that night. The dumplings and beer still warming my body nicely.

The morning arrived with a light dusting of snow on the ground, the day was young and full of the unknown. I rushed up the hill and stood atop the medieval wall, standing next to a fortification tower I looked upon Neumünster Abbey with its open court, tall black spire and leaf-less autumnal trees lining the curving Alzette River. Of all the cities I had seen thus far, Luxembourg City *felt* the most medieval. It was something about the walls and buildings which made it seem stuck in a time long ago. A place where one could imagine peasants wandering with contemplative eyes and armed guards using the slits in the walls for their bows. I rushed down into the open court and marveled at it all.

Following one of the winding walls, I ascended into stone turrets and all along watchtowers, following still until I ran out of ruins. I doubled back to follow the river and wound up amidst dreary colored houses looking up at a natural fortification wall with clouds hanging low completing the feel of a medieval city. Children were playing in a park as I ascended a zigzagging staircase and found myself away from the old town district and into the banking sector of one of the richest cities on Earth.

Soaring, multi-storied banks with gold-plated clocks stood tall at street corners, a semblance of the bountiful riches which lie within. The streets were lined with perfectly manicured trees and Christmas decorations hung just so contrasting boldly with the homeless backpacker vibe I was letting off. I walked along the pristine sidewalks, past people dressed in designer fashion, and we smiled warmly as we went our separate ways.

Next to a stone church I found a lively Christmas market with humble wooden sheds arranged in two rows. Holiday music was playing, the smell of mulled wine and gingerbread tainted the air with seasonal cheer while people of all ages leaned against chest high tables eating sausages and laughing with glee. A smile went across my face as I bit into a juicy bratwurst and drank a black coffee. Watching parents with their children made me miss the home that was waiting for me all too soon. I bought my first real gingerbread man and ate it as I set my sights on a hilltop fortress.

With my breathe fogging the air around me I hurried past the Cathedral Notre-Dame, stopped for a brief stare at the ceremonial guard outside the Palais Grand-Ducal, and through an archway with two medieval towers on either side. Climbing a dirt trail near my hostel, I passed through trees and brush and came to a grass opening with stone walls acting as retaining features to higher ground. I climbed over the first wall to find a second, this time higher, wall. Once that was climbed I came to the still higher, more elaborate fortifications of the Fortress of Luxembourg.

The view of Luxembourg City with the cranes adding on to the prosperous newer sectors seemed so far removed from the stone masonry of that higher elevation. The entire complex was empty of people and many of the towers were open. I climbed a few of them and took photos then finally came to the fortress-turned-museum of Musée Draï Eechelen. With rounded towers and a drained moat, the illusion of the medieval city was complete. I wandered the complex high on the hill, smiling and reflecting on where I was and how I had gotten there. It seemed like it had been so long since I first left America and jotted in my notebook, bulging with tickets and small keepsakes from cities previous, and wrote down some thoughts. The finality of my date of departure was hitting me and the impact of each day was palpable.

The morning came with a rush as my feet crunched through the dusting of snow on my way to the train station. A missed train used to bother me but by that point it seemed commonplace; I waited for the next one to show up without fret. The front page of papers in the train depot told the story of Brussels being on lockdown due to worries of a Paris-style terrorist attack. It seemed I was following the terrorist attacks, being only a few days behind the carnage of capital cities.

The countryside scrolled by like a kind of motion picture as we left the riches of Luxembourg City and ventured into rural Belgium. Pockets of snow laying white on fields and on country houses. People at train stops drained from monotony in a world I was so grateful to visit. A quick stop in Brussels, a train change here and there, and finally we arrive in Ghent.

It's amazing how different each city feels from one another. Sometimes its the smell, other times its the buildings or people or just a feeling. Ghent felt welcoming from the start as I walked through an average looking residential area. Hungry, I stopped into a small kebab shop. Throughout the trip I found kebab shops to be cheap and fast, perfect to gather my bearings and prepare for whatever lie ahead.

The man behind the counter had brown skin and an accent which was not Belgian. I ordered what I always ordered, then with a patronizing sneer he asked "where are you from?" It was a simple question but according to most Americans who have never left the country it is one which should be answered cautiously. Yet, after two months of travel I had found the question to be a gateway to interesting conversations and one I was always eager to answer truthfully. "I'm from the United States, how about you?"

Smiling that patronizing smirk, the man jeeringly said "I figured as much. I am from Turkey. My mother is from Afghanistan and my father is from Iraq. How does it feel being from a country who bullies countries so much smaller than them?" I was completely taken aback. Not believing what I had heard my defenses instantly went up and I felt naked. The small restaurant was filled with ten people, those of which were all white-skinned and who I believe were Belgian.

"I...I have no comment. I don't always agree with the politics of where I come from but I am not my country nor are you yours or your parents theirs. I don't think it is fair to judge someone on that."

As if waiting for me to finish, not dependent on the actual words I said, the Turkish man began spouting vitriolic hatred of America and how everyone from there was a capitalist brute who kills people and engages in wars which they have no business in being a part of and went on and on. I didn't know what to do. I had been in this new country for less than an hour, alone with no one who knew where I was getting berated by a man who knew nothing about me in a restaurant which I had entered only to buy a simple meal. "This is ridiculous" I said, "I'm leaving."

"No, no my friend" the man said laughing under his breath, "I will make you whatever you want, I didn't mean any harm." Hungry and embarrassed, I bought my kebab, sat at a window table and endured the stares from those around me. The kebab was amazing and I ate it hurriedly trying to think of what to say before I left.

With blood boiling and heart racing I walked up to the counter to give the man my tray back in a sign of peace. "I just wanted to say, one of my best friends back home is from Istanbul and he has told me numerous stories of the warmth and beauty of his home city." The man looked stunned as my cheeks burned red, "I don't think it was fair for you to berate me but I won't hold a grudge. Teşekkür ederim ("Thank you" in Turkish)." With a great pride I turned to leave only to have the man apologize for his behavior.

With a warm smile he asked me about my Turkish friend and how I knew Turkish. I accepted his apology but confessed I only knew simple phrases of the amazing language. The people in the restaurant, those who had earlier been laughing at me and where I came from, all had a confused look on their face as I left the small kebab restaurant. I walked along a waterway with pride in my heart. It would have been easy for me to tell the guy to "go fuck himself" and leave the shop with a burning rage but instead I kept a cool head and rose above my first bout of country shaming. I was surprised it took so long to rear its ugly head.

The strange incident didn't have much time to dwell in my thoughts as the commonplace buildings soon gave way to gothic architecture of which I had never seen. Amidst the old town district sat my hostel, a 13th century building on the edge of a canal. Entering the building was the stuff of every backpackers dreams. Centuries old wood gave the hallways an atmosphere of medieval brilliance. After being shown my bed I walked into the common room with overstuffed chairs and dim lights casting their glow on ceiling high windows looking out onto the canal. With heart skipping I hurried out into the dawn air and walked feverishly down the canal taking in as much of the architecture as I could.

Night fell quickly and the moon peeked through heavy clouds as young people snuggled on benches and photographers captured a beauty one can only find in Europe. I retired back to the hostel and set up my tablet next to a window to find it was happy hour at the bar. Working in the beer industry back in Oregon I had heard stories of the quality of Belgian beer. Having waited weeks, I ordered a beer brewed in Ghent and drank deeply.

The night was a blur of beer, talking with people from so many different countries, trying to write, failing miserably, comparing American versus Belgian craft beer with the bartender, and finally crashing into my pillow at some ridiculous hour trying to comprehend what kind of heaven-on-earth I had found.

Morning shone bright through a hangover-fueled headache as I walked to a window and realized where I was. With fast travel, and heavy drinking from the night previous, I had experienced a couple times the feeling of "which city am I in?" A strange feeling but one of which pride could be taken, or so I told myself.

As I was cobbling together breakfast from the layout in the kitchen, I overheard talk of a free walking tour of the old town district and I jumped at the chance. A group of ten of us wandered around the gothic area of the city for the better part of three hours. Our guide was a quirky Belgian man with an immense knowledge of the city and everyone was happy with the time spent.

After the tour we all went our separate ways and I found myself staring at a castle before walking down a long corridor with glow-in-the-dark painted bears ending at a canal. Leaning against the railing I heard a yell from across the water, I turned and saw a young guy with curly blonde hair and a plastic shopping bag waving his arm asking if I would join him on a bench. How could I say no?

The guy was French, probably in his early twenties with a joint in one hand and a cheap beer in the other. Without hesitation he offered me both but knowing my own dislike for weed I took a beer. We sat for a half hour chatting about where we came from, why we were in Ghent, and what our plans were for the evening.

It turned out he was backpacking around the northwest section of Europe before he was planning a trip to Australia for a long while. From what I gathered, he was a kid with rich parents and not many ambitions who jumped from city to city hitting raves and having anonymous encounters with the women who frequent such venues. He urged me to go with him to a rave that night but I declined, raving wasn't something I was into and after the night before I was looking forward to an early night.

We left the bench and walked around the old town district, drinking beers and talking about life. It was nice to have a conversation with a smart guy with no aspirations who lived in the moment. The entire walk he was stoned out of his mind and would stop mid-sentence to ask a big question. He would point up at the sky or grab his curly haired head and exclaim something ridiculous only to smile and take another drag from his ever-shortening joint.

    Night came and I thanked him for the beers and walked along a canal back to my hostel. It was Thanksgiving back home but no one in Europe could have cared less. I celebrated with a green soup and soft bread I bought for cheap at a local market earlier in the day. The allure of happy hour was too great and I talked to an American girl until late. We talked about how weird it was to celebrate a holiday in a foreign country and how our loved ones back home were gathering around a table eating good food and drinking in the warmth of the season. It was just another day in the world and we were lucky to have good beer and great company around us, the beer poured until late once again.

Before leaving the hostel the next morning I was told there was a bomb threat on the tramway; I would have to walk. People were becoming noticeably uneasy about the rash of terrorist related stories populating the news in such a short amount of time. With tensions high I went through town and found my way into the train station, armed guards with heavy body armor milling about with watchful eyes. Part of me saw these men and women as threats while the other part felt secure besides, who in their right mind would attack a building with that kind of fire power?

    The wonderfully sombre city of Bruges was only a twenty minute train ride away through the rain and heavy grey clouds of near-coastal Belgium. Arriving without any idea of where to go, I ventured down a dirt trail which led into a kind of convent area. Serene is the best word to describe the humble atmosphere acting as a place designed to inspire thought and meditation. Beautiful white swans were floating regally in a large pond in the middle of the small district, I watched them blissfully for some minutes before glimpsing a large tower through the bare trees and light fog.

I passed bright red door framed houses with ancient shingles and cobblestones glistening from the on-again-off-again rain as I neared the towers. From the minimal research I had done between bouts of sipping on good beer in Ghent, I knew those towers were important. The architecture was stunning and the people sparse as I walked over canal bridges which seemed numerous, a bit of a Venice feel, minus the sunshine and smell of pizza.

As if looking at a postcard, I found myself in the main square of the old town district looking up at one of the large towers, a belfry to be exact. Jutting up high above anything else surrounding, the medieval bell tower was like nothing I had ever seen before. Mesmerized, I walked into the courtyard behind it and stood in awe. That feeling of being dumbfounded by the mixture of architecture, atmosphere, and location never seemed to dull; whenever those three elements came together it was like getting kicked in the head in the best possible way.

After I picked my mouth up off the ground I walked back into the square and was amazed, again, by the beautifully Belgian architecture of the buildings surrounding it. With sharp edges and ascending steps, the facades of buildings in that corner of the world is all its own. The colors were fantastic as well, one building was even painted pink, a classy pink which was the perfect mixture.

Once my awe wore off I walked the five minutes through winding streets, past another belfry, and through a complete cobblestone reconstruction zone to get to my hostel. Walking in, I was greeted by a Belgian man who could only be described as apathetic. He didn't give two shits and he wanted everybody to know it. We exchanged pleasantries and as I was signing paperwork he bluntly exclaimed, "I'm surprised you didn't cancel your plans to come to Belgium. So many Americans are doing that." It seemed like a strange way to invite me to his city so we talked a bit about what he meant. "The terrorists. They seem to have found their way to Belgium," he said with a serious face.

We talked about why the terrorists would want to populate Belgium, why people shouldn't change their plans just because a bomb might go off, and how strange it was for me, an American, to be that close to real-life terrorism. As an isolationist country, for reasons of geography or by choice, we have avoided the proximity to terrorism with a few grand exceptions. But, being on a continent or, better yet, in a governing body such as the European Union where everyone, no matter how differing their politics or religion, can intermix was a different feeling. It felt like anyone could attack anything at anytime and no amount of border control or lockdown would fix that. The man behind the counter was no longer apathetic and was great conversation until a fellow backpacker walked in and I made my way up to my room.

A walking tour was starting soon after I had checked-in and followed the group of dapper looking backpackers to a pub to start it off. We walked around every historical part of Bruges including the convent with the swans I had seen earlier, saw a church proclaiming to contain a vial of Christ's blood brought back from the crusades, learned a bit about Flanders and the history of the power that once was in Bruges, sampled Belgian chocolate at a traditional chocolatiers shop, and ended with a tour of a beer museum overlooking the main square complete with two of Bruges' finest beverages.

With night beginning to fall I wanted to get out of the tourist-filled town square. During the tour I had heard there were traditional windmills on the edge of town and set out looking for them following a long canal with beautiful houses lining it. With the lights of streetlamp illuminating the low hanging clouds, I found a path which took me past a few windmills situated on mounds of Earth. With no one around, the mills seemed eerie and inactive, a welcome reprieve from the bustle of the day. I stuck headphones in my ears and walked back along a canal toward my hostel, I told myself tonight would be a restful, early-to-bed kind of night.

Nothing could have been further from the truth. As I opened the hostel door I was met with a cacophony of upbeat music, chatter, and the man behind the counter holding a beer, "tonight we are having a beer tasting, you should join us!" How could I resist?

With a quick change of clothes, I hustled down to the common room just in time for the get-to-know-your-roommates kind of period. The large couch I was sitting on was soon jammed with five people my age talking about all manner of travel, careers, school, and general ambitions in life. The girl next to me was Canadian, in Bruges for a business trip, and was looking to have a fun night before she went home the next day. We talked for the entire hour until a young woman who I could only describe as 'classy slutty' rang a small bell and began the nights festivities.

There would be six different styles of Belgian beer, half brewed in Bruges. We would get a 12-ounce glass of each and we would discuss how we liked each successive beer as we went on. After working in the craft beer industry for a couple years, I was extremely excited. Within our group of ten, which was gaining people exponentially as time went on, there was quite a bit of beer knowledge to pass around. After the third beer most of us were using the twenty minutes between beers to yell over the top of one another, make jokes, and divulge ridiculous tidbits about ourselves; in short we were getting drunk.

The beers kept pouring and the crowd got bigger and hosts started drinking, by the end it was chaos and the entire room was bulging with drunken hilarity and fun. It was midnight before the beers were finished and the room split into two groups. The first group, mostly full of a group of German guys, a few especially drunk Americans, and girls who wanted to dance, had decided to find a club which the hosts guaranteed would be a good time. The rest of us, maybe eight people, wanted more of a laid back environment and decided to wander into the old town square to see what was available.

The five minute walk from before was now a disaster, it would have been easier herding cats through a maze then it was guiding eight twenty-something backpackers in a straight direction at midnight on a weekday in Bruges.

Once in the square we all decided on an Irish bar, found a table, and ordered more drinks. Beer began to flow and conversation took wild turns as we all forgot our inhibitions and drank pint after pint of beers from all over the world. People made vows to get married, others exchanged phone numbers and added each other as friends on social media, but in the end we all got to know each other at that most primitive level of drunkenness.

As the night wore on people dropped out of the bar one by one. I left with a couple other guys once the bartender began stacking barstools on tables. After all the drinking I had done thus far on my trek through Europe I was in much better shape then some of my comrades. Somehow we made it back to the hostel in one piece only to find a few couples making out and groping each other in dark corners as we stumbled up the staircase. It was almost four as I climbed into my bunk having drank more beers than I could remember, or care to for that matter.

Morning came with a dull roar as my alarm shouted. After four hours of sleep and who knows how many drinks my body was feeling less than amazing. A quick shower helped ease the pain and as I walked back into my room to pack my bags a young American walked in looking worse than how my head felt. After a few minutes of talking to him I recognized him from the beer tasting from the night previous.

Apparently, he was part of the "go to the club" party and drank way too much and ended up pissing on the door of a church around four in the morning. The local police picked him up and threw him in jail for the night but not before charging him a fine and threatening to kick him out of the country. The young American didn't seem too upset, he had aspirations of becoming a writer one day and it would make a great story.

Walking to the bus station in that promising early morning glow I reflected on the night before. It was days like those where I felt sad at spending less than 24 hours in a city. Had I really experienced what the city had to offer? I didn't have time to dwell on those kinds of questions. My tickets were bought, bags were packed, and a form of transportation was ready to take me to a new land with new experiences and novel things to see. There was always time to travel slow and experience things to their fullest, it was rapid travel which can only happen when one is young.

The train was traveling back to Ghent, I was reading a book about American politics in the 1970's, and a young man across from me was looking at me over a book about Che Guevara. The man, actually about my age, and I started talking about our time in Bruges. It turned into an amazing conversation which led to talks of other things and future and past travels. The train stopped in Ghent and it turned out we were both on the same bus to Amsterdam.

Excited to be in a city I had already been, I hurriedly showed my companion the old town district with its gothic architecture and talked about all manner of things including the drunk/stoned guy who I had talked to only days previous which he countered with similar stories of what seemed to be a template for the "drunk and stoned guy" everyone has met at least once in life. With a lapse in time, we rushed to our green bus with the word AMSTERDAM shining on its destination plate and leaped aboard with minutes to spare.

The American and I talked about a lot in the four and a half hours it took us to get to Amsterdam. It turned out my companion had grown up in California. Once he finished high school he had tried his hand at college, partied too hard and decided to take a break and travel. He decided rural Mexico would be the most appropriate place for a young man in his situation so he packed his bags, drained his bank account, not tell his parents, and head off to who-the-fuck-knows Mexico.

The times were great at the beginning, everything was cheaper and the girls were dark and beautiful. Before long the money ran out and he looked for work in the fields soon finding employment on some crop out in the middle of nowhere. Times were great once again until he got sick. It was pneumonia. Pneumonia in the lungs of a young man who no one with any kind of insurance knew where he was. Those around him took him to a local doctor who did the best they could which resulted in a two month stay in a bed from complications, fever, and infection. The guy grew up during that period and gained clarity on the meaning of life and how precious each day truly is.

He made his way back to the United States, found a well paying job, saved up just enough money to travel to Europe and now he sat next to me. I asked what he would do with a story like that and he said he wanted to write a book, a book which was nearly complete.

After many stories and pondering of the meaning of life and what the future would bring us, the man who had gotten pneumonia and I went our separate ways once the bus stopped in Amsterdam. I had only thirty hours before I moved on, I hadn't done really any research on what to see or do, but I was in Amsterdam and ready to make the most of it.

As with so many times before, the first objective was to find the hostel I had booked the day previous. Using a new map app on my phone, I quickly found how to get to my bed for the night. I wound through the downtown area, past the Red Light District, through the Christmas decorations bright and jolly, and through the busy Amsterdam central station. It turned out my hostel was on the other side of the river from the central station so I boarded a ferry, made my way across, and found my comfortable hostel with ease. With a quick turnaround I was back in the heart of Amsterdam in the early part of the evening amidst the glow of lights and throngs of people ready to be washed with the experiences the city had to offer.

My first stop, as I imagine is the case for most young men, was the Red Light District. I had no intention of engaging in any kind of sexual act but my curiosity for the infamous area was too strong to not see what there was to offer. Within a short amount of time I was unimpressed. From stories I now know to be embellished, I was expecting naked women in windows caressing their sensitive parts and propositioning men with zest and vigor. Instead, women exuding a classy vibe sat semi-awkwardly behind glass windows knocking, yes knocking, at young men such as myself hoping for them to show interest, exchange payment, and be allowed behind closed doors to engage in extremely defined sexual acts. It didn't take me long to understand the game and I walked up and down the streets, passing countless windows with women for all types of fetishes and smiled sheepishly at the knocks.

After walking for some time I stopped in front of a window advertising different strains of marijuana and began thinking of how I should spend my thirty hours in Amsterdam. It didn't take long to decide on the weed allure.

Throughout my life I have smoked weed numerous times. I'm definitely not a recreational pot smoker but I have had periods where I've smoked two or three times a month. Once I reached college I began drinking more than smoking until I gave up marijuana all together, except for the random college parties here and there where I would have two hits then get extremely paranoid and ridicule myself for imbibing in the purple haze.

Despite this information, I decided it fitting to get high in Amsterdam. I walked up and down the streets looking for the place I deemed fit to fix my craving and finally settled on a green-signed coffeeshop with a conspicuous marijuana leaf on the window. As soon as I walked in I saw a table full of eighteen year old girls each taking turns hitting a three foot tall hookah, each laughing maniacally after they had done so.

I had never bought weed in public before so when I bellied up to the bar and two extremely stereotypical Jamaican guys with a Rastafari-vibe came over to help me I began sweating and was beyond nervous. They guided me through the complex menu of weights and letters until I settled on a piece of dessert called a "Space Cake." I told the guys behind the counter I was a lightweight but they both assured me it was a *mild* blend and would not make me freak out or get *too* high. Trusting them I bought the cupcake-shaped cake, took it to a corner table and began slowly and deliberately consuming the edible.

From experience, I knew edibles were dangerous. Smoking the herb was more immediate in its effects while eating something with marijuana in it takes a bit of time to get absorbed into the bloodstream so the high can come on hours later without any real warning. It must have been the atmosphere of the day-glo painted walls, the arcade vibe in the back of the building, or the simple act of being in a city such as Amsterdam but in the end I ate all of the cake in a matter of forty minutes. I left the coffeehouse feeling completely normal, put on my headphones, and walked along the canals of Amsterdam underneath the lights of the enormous Christmas displays hanging above.

The canals were beautiful in the night with little phrases such as "love" or "peace" or "hope" traced in twinkle lights above bridges with couples holding hands and snuggling into each other as they explored the streets in that late November night. My music was hitting me on all cylinders as the weed began peaking my senses. The lights grew brighter and my hands felt lighter as I continued to walk up and down the streets, into shops selling interesting clothes and into glass shops with some of the most intricate glassware I had ever seen.

About an hour after leaving the coffeehouse my music began making me paranoid and I felt like people were staring at me, judging me. The lights I had found beautiful not long before seemed glaring and much too bright for any sane person to handle. My body felt like a balloon too full of air and my lungs were too inflated. Paranoia began to swell from deep within and my brain began to experience The Fear, the all too familiar brute which saturates my brain with all things terrible and disparaging. The Fear is the reason I stopped smoking weed entirely, it was one thing to have to deal with it by myself in my apartment but it was an entirely different beast to manage in the bustling city streets of one of the most traveled cities in the world.

Trying to collect myself I tugged my headphones out of my ears and stood next to a glass window with an enormous poster of marijuana plants behind it. A nagging feeling from deep in my brain told me I had to get to my hostel, it was now a mission. The strength of the high just kept coming. As I walked through the throngs of people on my way to the central station it felt like everyone in the Netherlands was looking right into my eyes. People seemed to ooze past me and the lights from the decorations above had a strange, ugly sheen I had never seen before.

The central station was an absolute nightmare of people with their eyes and security guards sizing me up, knowing something was amiss. Somehow I made it to the ferry, clamored on and found a corner seat and tried not looking conspicuous, I'm sure the farthest thing I could have seemed at that point. The ferry docked and I hurried toward the hostel, past the doors, through the common room filled with fellow backpackers playing games and drinking cool drinks. I found my room, my bed, took off my shoes in what felt like an eternity, curled into bed, and watched a romantic comedy all while my head was reeling with the effects of the *"mild"* Space Cake from the Jamaican Rastafarian's in the green-labeled coffeeshop in the heart of Amsterdam.

My eyes opened the next morning and I sat up in my bottom bunk with head spinning and eyes unable to focus. A shower and heavy breakfast helped to rid my brain of the cobwebs but even as I walked into the crisp morning air and made my way across the drizzling river my body didn't feel right. I was experiencing a marijuana hangover, the same kind of feeling which drove me to quit smoking weed altogether years ago.

    I walked into the city center from the night before and saw the gross remnants of the party city. Vomit lay in puddles in corners and the smell of urine was strong in different sections, the ugly underbelly of a city which prides itself in sin. Making my way through the Red Light District I saw an opportunity to take a few photos, not of the women but of the red lights which surround their glass enclosures.

Turning down a particular street where a large church runs parallel to a few women's windows, I snapped a photo of the interesting juxtaposition. Before I knew what was happening, a prostitute, maybe in her late 50's, ran out of her door in skimpy lingerie yelling at me in a thick Dutch accent "GIVE ME THAT FUCKING CAMERA!!!" She was furious and, not wanting confrontation, I walked hastily the opposite direction. I turned down this street and that thinking she would have some kind of pimp or guard following after me but that may have been the weed talking from the night before.

The majority of that day was spent walking through the main centers of Amsterdam, past a large park next to the Van Gogh museum where there was a protest and concert happening. I tried finding windmills on the edge of town but they were too far away. In the end I walked non-stop for the entire day until around eight that night I found the bus depot.

The overnight bus to London loaded in the dark, rainy night. With all the excitement from the last few days it didn't take long to find a comfortable position and let my heavy eyelids close from exhaustion. Twelve hours later I would be in London, I could never have guessed what lie between Amsterdam and that famous metropolis.

Chapter 17

United Kingdom

The lights from the bus shone dully on the back roads stretching from Amsterdam on into the French countryside. Sleep came easy that night, a luxury when traveling by cramped bus, and I vaguely remember waking at random spots and watching the nothingness of late night road travel. Around three in the morning the bus came to a halt next to a brightly lit building and a man in a tidy uniform boarded and began sternly telling us to get off the bus.

Sharply aroused from a deep sleep I grabbed my passport and stuffed my beanie over my long, unwashed hair and assembled into the line of weary travelers shuffling along the spine of the bus. This line continued into the border patrol office building and we snaked around the rope barriers waiting as the people in front of us got grilled as to where they were going and why they were going there.

The patrol agents were efficient and made their way quickly through the group of people in front of me. When it was my turn, I stepped confidently forward and faced the exceptionally neat, grey mustachioed older man. He asked for my passport and stood staring at it and my face, whatever he saw he wasn't pleased. The man began asking questions at a rapid pace trying to catch me in a lie. "What business do you have in England?" "How will you get back to the United States?" "What were you doing in Amsterdam?"

Trying to keep my cool as best as I could I answered them as earnestly as possible. It seemed no matter the answer I gave, the more curious of me he became. "Do you have the ticket from Iceland to the United States?"

I answered in the affirmative but he tasked me with showing him the ticket. "It is on my phone and I don't have cell phone reception," I said with a bit of sweat starting under my arms.

"Use this password, we have all night to wait," he said with a grin.

The next five minutes seemed like hours as I stood there with hands shaking trying to search my email not being able to find the boarding pass which would take me home. By that point all of my bus-mates had been passed through and an entirely new set of passengers was filling up behind me. Other border patrol agents had picked up on the uneasiness I was supposedly putting off and were exchanging glances in my direction in what I can only assume means "alright, its about time we put the gloves on and tell this hippie punk to bend over!"

Thankfully, I found the boarding pass, the stern patrol agent gave me one last, cold look of disapproval and stamped my passport with a forceful thud. I walked outside in the early morning darkness of that sea-side village and boarded my bus, every set of eyes watching me as I walked past them to my seat. I was shaking with anxiety.

Soon our bus boarded a ferry, we all got off and milled about as we crossed the English Channel from Calais, France to Dover, United Kingdom. Once in the UK our bus departed the ferry and made its way through the south of England in the early morning glow of day. I found myself staring out the window watching as small towns passed by with signs in English. It hadn't occurred to me until later how nice it was to not have to translate signs and announcements made over the intercoms. Many, if not most, of the places I had been in the past two and a half months were quite accommodating with their English signage but it hadn't been its first language. I found myself enjoying the language barrier. It was nice to not be catered to just because I was an American or that I spoke English.

By eight in the morning the bus stopped along the River Thames and I walked onto the sidewalks of one of my most desired destinations in all the world, we were in jolly ole London.

With my awkward pack and tired eyes I set out to find a cafe. The streets were filled with the English accent we all know and the black cabs sped around like they do in the movies. I found a small cafe and ordered an English breakfast tea with milk, of which I had never taken, and sat at a window looking out at a small farmer's market and the colorful characters partaking in the joy underneath the grey clouds.

With a slight game plan in mind, I downed the tea and headed off in the direction of Buckingham Palace. Amidst the throngs of vacationers with high white socks and more fanny packs than had been expected, I watched the guards in the tall furry hats stand at attention in front of the magnificent home to the royals. Walking away from the palace I saw Big Ben peeking through the leafless trees and a flitter went through my heart. I hurried along through St. James Park along the Princess Diana Walkway, passed so many mothers and fathers with small children enjoying the park and made me think of home and the future which was so uncertain.

Before long I was standing in front of Westminster Abbey and her gorgeous gothic architecture. It was hard not to join the thousands of people in the city in becoming a complete tourist. I walked across the complex and looked up at Big Ben chiming and took in the walls of Parliament. With head swiveling, I crossed Westminster Bridge, found a cheap lunch and ate under the London Eye. Next was crossing London Bridge, looking up in awe at The Shard, taking photos on Tower Bridge and walking along the edges of the Tower of London.

Through the business district with well-groomed financial people in their dark colors and nice shoes, along Oxford Street with the flashing lights and street performers and so many people choking the sidewalks. By accident I found Baker Street and walked around trying to find the Sherlock Holmes Museum which had been one of my top ten most anticipated museums of the entire trip.

With phone map in hand, I left the bustling inner city and hustled to the quieter South Hampstead district where I was assured my hostel would be. After miles of walking I eventually found my hostel well into the night, checked in, found some expensive food, and settled into the common room. While in the kitchen, I met an Australian who was standing by the sink eating hamburger raw from the packaging. My eyes must have shown my worry for his GI tract as he assured me it was often how he consumed his meat. We began laughing and a hippie girl from England came in to make her food and we all talked for a while about travel and sights to see in London and how expensive everything was. Once our food was done we departed and never saw each other again. Truly one of the beauties of hostel living is the ability to make extremely short-term friends which ignite brilliantly but fade out before the light reaches its full potential.

The next morning I woke in the bottom bunk of my cramped room with men and women snoring loudly from all corners. Only having that one full day to explore London I raced through the hostel and was so thankful to walk-out into sunshine and blue skies. First, it was to the Abbey Road crosswalk made famous by the Beatles. Not too far from my hostel I made it there rather quickly and was dumbfounded when I realized, it is just a crosswalk. Like so many sights throughout the world the hype was in the history of the people and regions not in the actual thing itself. Without being perturbed I waited for a break in traffic, of which there were few, and I walked across the same stretch of road as the Fab Four.

    With no real itinerary for the day I set myself on getting to higher ground. A quick search on my phone showed

Primrose Hill as a nearby spot so I walked past stereotypical English houses with their brick exteriors and classy atmosphere surrounding the whole lot. Primrose Hill offered a decent view of the distant downtown London sights. I sat amongst the people and watched dogs playing and children running around in the grass. The barking and the laughter made the blue skies and the sunshine of the day so much more relaxing. I walked down through The Regents Park and back on to Baker Street.

The Sherlock Holmes Museum satisfied my childhood love of the famous detective and I took more photos of wax mannequins than I thought I ever would have in life. From there I walked through SoHo then down to Piccadilly Circus and was caught in the madness of Trafalgar Square with its columns and lions and ticker tape horse skeleton. With violin music playing in my ears I walked back down to the Thames and leaned against rails taking in the view of the London skyline. It was in London where I was immersed in so many postcard-moments, images I had grown up seeing, where I could be anywhere in the city doing nothing at all and be amazed. All I wanted to do was to walk around the city and look up at the mixture of historical and modern buildings, a perfect conglomeration of the past and present, hear the traditional English accents mixed with every kind of accent the world has to offer.

I walked back to my hostel that night drained from the miles walked but also drained from a profound sense of finality. It was December 1st and I was to complete my trip on December 11th. It so happened, amidst these thoughts of home and finality, that that night was a Christmas movie night. Sitting in the common room with a bunch of strangers we drank the cheapest beer we could find and watched movies set in American cities with American accents and I think all of us, no matter the nationality, missed the homes we came from.

As most travel days do, the morning started with an intense rush. Confident in my travel ability I bought the bus ticket to the airport and headed down to where the bus would arrive. The time on the ticket came and went and just as I was about to give up I watched my bus pull up to the sidewalk a distance away from where I was standing. In a kind of repeat from Copenhagen, I began chasing after the bus only to have it pull out into traffic just as I had gotten close to it. Frantic, I sprinted back up to my hostel, bought another bus ticket, and stood in the correct waiting area. This time the plan worked and the bus took me to the airport, I went through security without question, and was soon boarding a $16 flight from London to Copenhagen.

The two hour flight was beautiful in the early December sunlight as the ground sped below us. We landed in Denmark just before dusk, went through customs with a simple smile, and took the tram to the central station. It felt so strange walking out into the City Hall Square of Copenhagen. It had been weeks since I was standing in that exact spot, the same spot I shared with a great friend on the last day of his trip and the first day of my solo trip.

With eyes feeling wet I walked past sights I had already seen and a flood of images and stories and people I had met along the trip came rushing into my head. The fun part of the trip was over. Up until then there was no plan, there was only whatever I wanted to do whenever I wanted to do it. I had always known the final day would be December 11th but it always seemed like a fragment of a dream, never to really come into reality but only to hang ethereal above all of the great experiences and feelings of weightless enjoyment that can only come with living each day to its fullest.

After walking for some distance I arrived at my hostel not being able to recall any of what I had walked past on the way there. Still in some kind of blur, I was shown my room, changed, and sat in the common room with a cold beer and began looking through pictures. I went back to the photos I had taken when I had first arrived in Europe then just kept cycling through.

The various landscapes swept by representing the imaginary line I had drawn across the continent. Looking through those photos was impactful, it put into perspective all that I had seen in such a short amount of time. I closed my eyes that night with visions of mountain tops and Italian canals, people's faces and artwork, my mind wandered down the rabbit hole of my experiences in the past weeks trying to make some kind of sense of the enormity of all.

In the end sleep came like it always does and puts an end to yet another day, another day which we will never be able to live again.

Chapter 18

Denmark Pt. 2

Morning came with a kind of melancholy; it was the first time I had retraced my steps and wound up back in a city which I had already been. This time I was alone.

The excitement with which I had explored Copenhagen months earlier had gone and as I sat up in the bottom bunk of an empty room in the heart of Denmark I felt a kind of overwhelming dread began to wash over me. In a couple days I would be getting on a boat bound for the end of my journey. There would be no more endless traveling, no more chaos, no more adventure. I would be going back to a life I had purposefully abandoned, one which I had severed most ties as far as jobs or prospects for the future were concerned.

I thought of my family and how they were all I had left back home. They would be overjoyed to welcome me back from my crazy adventure, one which they did not fully understand, but the thought of going back was a departure from the intense self-centeredness which I had been cultivating for almost three months. I think that is why I was feeling so down leading up to getting on the ship to Iceland. At the same time there was adventure in that last push, the only way to leave a trip of such magnitude.

Over coffee, I edited photos and jotted notes, eavesdropped on a conversation in a language I couldn't understand, then left the hostel and began walking in the rain. I trudged through the sombre buildings typical of Scandinavian cities, into the downtown area, past Christiania with the "dope fiends," along the canal with Poseidon and his crew, the multi-colored buildings of Nyhavn, Tivoli, the rush of the Centraal Market, through an indoor farmers market, and made it back to the hostel at the end of the day for happy hour.

I drank beers in the corner of the common room that night looking at the weather forecast for the North Sea and felt twinges of anxiety and exhilaration, there was a monstrous storm hammering Iceland and the Faroe Islands. The entire trip up until that point was footloose and without time constraints but now, with a storm above me, I had delicate schedules to keep and Mother Nature was on the other side ready to make chaotic what I had hoped to be steady.

The train left the main station, the same station which months earlier I had missed my bus to Hamburg, and we rambled on north, crossing many bodies of water, finally arriving to Aarhus midday. By this point in the trip I had given up all hope of planning what I was going to do as far as sights went and walked out of the train station to the docks nearby. Coastal cities drive me crazy in the best possible way. The way they smell, the atmosphere, the ships, it all comes together in a kind of magical way which is irresistible. I think in some capacity it is because they act as a stepping off point. Every body of water is a journey waiting to take place. Find a vessel, take the ride, and the unpredictable nature of open water will set a person free. I stood at that dock for nearly an hour looking at a pristine rainbow and thinking about what tomorrow would bring.

It wasn't hard to find my hostel, I checked in, and wandered the streets aimlessly trying to pass time. The weather to the north of me and the uncertainty it presented put me in a kind of headspace which preoccupied any thoughts other than travel, sights could only be an afterthought. With headphones blaring trying to drown the anxiety, I walked past the university, down along the Latin Quarter, found a used bookstore with a decent English section and bought L'Amour's *Education of a Wandering Man*, past churches, a cemetery, along canals, saw a Christmas tree atop a fort's turret, and wandered around a giant supermarket before making my way back to the hostel.

I found the common area of the hostel occupied with a group of middle eastern men, all nice and talkative and asking if I knew where the best clubs were. They left leaving a smell of mixed cologne and testosterone behind them as I opened a beer brewed in the city of Aarhus and read the book I had just bought. The book tells the story of an aspiring author going on adventures and using the knowledge picked up along the way to carve out an existence as a writer in the Western genre.

When I read it a couple years earlier I had no idea where my life would end up, sitting at a dining room table in Denmark was something I could have never predicted.

The alarm rang with shrill clang at 6:45 the following morning, it was travel day. Frantic, I gathered my things, stuffed my long hair up into my beanie, and rushed to the train station. The train to Hirtshals left at 7:48. I changed trains three times each descending in quality and amount of people aboard. The final train shook as it reached its destination, the doors opened and I felt the fury of the storm raging to the north, there was no way a ship would be leaving the northern tip of Denmark that day.

Four years previous I had worked as a deckhand on a commercial salmon fishing boat in southeast Alaska. It was summer so the weather wasn't crazy but as the season began to close, around the end of September, the sea was getting angry. It was during this time when I had my first experience with rough seas. There were times the wind would be so heavy that the crest of the waves would peak in white then the water would get whipped away by the wind. Other times we would be fishing in seas much too rough for our forty foot, wooden boat and I would be looking up at a wave, I would rush to the other side, the wave would crash forcefully, I would rush back, then the other side would get hit, all the while the boat was listing deeply to one side then the other.

It was because of those experiences that I knew no ship with a captain in his right mind would leave port on the kind of day Hirtshals was having. I tried reassuring myself, "these people are descended from Vikings. If there were ever any culture who could do it, it would be them!"

Ducking my head into the intense, howling wind I struggled over toward the stone breakers to get a better look at the severity of the sea. In the bay, behind the large breaker, boats were bobbing and rocking like toys in a bath. Beyond the breakers the brown sea was breaking savagely with the same white cresting waves I had seen in Alaska when things got gnarly. I took a quick video of the horrendous sight, mostly to check myself later, and turned back to the road completely empty of human life. A supermarket was nearby so I went in for shelter and supplies.

With a few bags of groceries I found the point of departure for my ferry and began to walk. The wind was relentless as I walked through the small town. I came to the spot on my phone's map which was the main ferry office but was met with an all encompassing wire fence. Discouraged and welling with anxiety I walked back to the supermarket, the only place which seemed to have people in it. Once out of the wind I began to think.

I had travelled all the way to the tip of Denmark, a place not on any tourist map and with no accommodation that time of year, and I was alone with my only means of leaving closed by a fence and a gale force wind. After some minutes of intense self-loathing I gathered myself and found an employee of the store.

The man was probably in his late thirties with a full black beard and inviting face. I explained my situation to him and without missing a beat he took me into the back and dialed a local taxi driver he knew. In a few minutes I was getting driven to the correct ferry office by a large man with a thick accent who charged an exorbitant fee for the few miles driven. Regardless, I thanked the man for the ride and walked up the stairs of the office waiting to see what the verdict would be.

With wind rattling the windows, I walked up to the desk, showed the clerk my boarding pass to the ferry, and was relieved when she accepted it. There would be a few hour delay in departure but she assured me the ship would leave that day. Ecstatic, I sat amongst the motley crew of people, mostly Scandinavian, and tried to keep my mind off the howling wind just on the other side of the windows.

As the hours passed, more and more people filled the lobby. Some were Danish, some were Icelandic, one man was from the middle east, and I was the only native English speaker in the room of about forty adults and children. Months ago this would have caused alarm but after all I had been through being the only American was no big deal.

Hours passed by with no confirmed word. Rumors spread amongst the waiting passengers of delays and cancellations but no one would officially announce the fate of the ferry passengers. It had begun to get dark and children were falling asleep in makeshift beds laid out on the cold floor of the ferry lobby. With windows rattling at a higher frequency a timid voice came over the loudspeaker first in Danish then in English explaining all the passengers would be ferried to a city an hour away where the ferry awaited our loading. With a confused chatter we all gathered our belongings, boarded an old fashioned bus with little heat, and started south in the night.

Silence filled the bus as our group of strangers were hauled along the dark roads. The lights became more numerous and soon we found ourselves in the small town of Frederikshavn parked in front of a large dock with multiple ferries in various states of loading and unloading. A military official walked onto our bus and told us which ferry to load, we quietly obeyed and walked through the cold night's air toward the shimmering behemoth awash with yellow light.

    I walked through the massive cargo hold already stocked with all-terrain vehicles and large crates, up flights of stairs, and onto the carpeted floors of a passenger ferry. The entire ship was devoid of any kind of human sound, it was like I was alone on my own ship. Looking at my ticket I quickly found my cabin, a dual bunk bed room with a friendly artist from Iceland sitting atop the bed I was about to choose. We spoke briefly before I left to explore the odd sensation of an empty ship. After exploring each floor I found myself walking into the bar. In the corner was a guy about my age looking out the window.

    We struck up a conversation and it turned out he was raised in the Faroe Islands and was using the ferry to get back home to his family for the holidays. "You have nothing to worry about," he said with almost perfect English. "This ferry supplies the Faroe Islands and eastern Iceland with essential supplies, theres nothing that'll stop her from making the trip. We may arrive a bit late but in all the years I've travelled this route, I've never seen it be cancelled."

    With that my nerves were relaxed. From his backpack he produced two cans of warm beer. We drank deeply from the elixir until three in the morning chatting about everything under the sun. It was conversations like those which meant the most to me. Alone one minute and connecting deeply with a stranger from a different land with a completely different set of views and beliefs but in the end able to connect on multiple levels. During those hours the ship remained deathly quiet, only the forklifts outside our ship's walls were moving and making any kind of noise.

    I walked into my cabin and was greeted with three men snoring and scratching. The bottom bunk was filled with my backpack and groceries, I pushed them aside and slept hard. According to the screen in the main lobby the ship would sail the next day. All of the anxiety I had felt in the days leading up to that bunk were gone. Any kind of schedule or itinerary had no relevance anymore. The anticipation of adventure was too great to worry about anything but the present because only when you are truly living can you forget the past and future and live in the second to second.

Chapter 19

North Atlantic

Note:
What follows is taken directly out of the author's journal.

12.5.2015

10:15 PM

I didn't think I would do this but here it is. A real-time journal about a small but crazy important piece of my three month trip. Right now I'm on a ferry, an empty ferry, in a small town in Denmark called Frederikshavn. The wind has been blowing a gale from the moment I got off the train this morning and I had been sure, since that moment, the trip to Iceland had been cancelled. The good part, it's not cancelled. The bad part, it's not cancelled *yet*. But why am I on a ferry in Denmark? Why aren't I on a beach in Portugal soaking up sun and getting ready to spend a relaxing flight back home from Lisbon? Because this is what I do.

Back in the very beginning of this trip, somewhere in Scandinavia with Reed, maybe Finland, I had heard about a ferry which left Denmark and went to Iceland and instantly I was hooked. That was around three months ago and I didn't act on it. December was a long way away and I didn't want to book anything more than a couple days in advance to secure the freedom of the trip. I let it go and told myself I probably wouldn't go through with it and left it at that. Unfortunately, that is not how my brain works and I've been thinking about it ever since.

But why Iceland? Why do I have to go back up to a frozen tundra in December? That is a whole other story involving last minute ticket buying in New York before the trip even began. Due to certain events I was forced to buy a return ticket with Icelandair which, as one can guess, mostly operates out of Iceland. So back in America I made the rash decision to fly back home from Reykjavik in December without thinking of the ramifications that would entail. Fast forward to Italy and the conversation begins to turn to make a full circle.

As I said before, my brain works in strange ways, some would say arrogant, self-absorbed ways but I say "strange." Once an idea which sounds beyond the norm gets into my head I begin to expand it. The expansion only stops once the idea morphs into something so extreme that few other sane people would go through with said idea. As soon as this happens the idea starts to become a reality. Here's what I mean. I had a simple problem: get to Iceland to fly out the

11th of December. Simple solution: fly out of any major airport in mainland Europe to Reykjavik and catch the flight no problem. The issue with that plan is the ease by which it can be accomplished. There is no story behind it. No thrill. The only thing exciting about it are the locations from which I would be flying. Most people would do this plan, and they should. It's stress free, it's easy, there is virtually no risk. This is where my off-kilter brain takes over.

Why take a direct flight when there is a ferry involved? I would be going from the tip of Denmark to the Faroe Islands then off to eastern Iceland in *December*. What are the problems with that? For one, the North Atlantic is an unforgiving bitch on a good day and I'm going to be heading up there when she's really ready to give her all. Two, I won't even be going to Reykjavik but to a super small town on the exact opposite side of the country. Three, there are few reliable means of transportation to get from eastern to western Iceland. And to top all this off, I had to sign an agreement that essentially said "if weather prohibits the ferry from making the trip and you can't get to your destination it's on you and there is no refund." So there's that.

All my idiocy aside, from what I understand there is a hell of a bout of bad weather in the exact direction we are supposed to be going. According to a group of apathetic ship workers we are staying put for tonight then tomorrow at 10:30 AM we are heading up to Hirtshals, the place we were supposed to leave from, loading cargo trucks and such for about an hour, then starting the trek to the Faroe Islands. The weather for the morning looks okay and if it stays like that then Iceland is a go but if not then we turn around and head back to Denmark. The ferry has to be back by Wednesday night so there is a deadline. Not a bad thing since that gives me time to book a last minute, and expensive, ticket home...but at least it will be home.

Anyway, that's how I got into this madness of an adventure, I wouldn't have it any other way. We shall see what the morning brings.

12.6.2015

10:14 AM

I was up until three this morning talking to a guy born and raised in the Faroe Islands. Multiple times during our talk he reassured me this ferry NEVER cancels. Apparently I booked the most resilient ferry in the fleet since its main purpose is a cargo liner. The entire bottom section is one giant hold for shipping containers and such and is the main life blood for the Faroe Islands and Iceland for supplies. This made me extremely happy last night after he said it and I really believe him. The only issue, the crew of the ferry do not seem nearly as confident as he is. Everyone I ask gives me really spotty answers and they always end with a shrug and "that is, if we *make* it to Iceland." Not the best thing to say to someone who is heading there but whatever.

On a less pessimistic note, this is the first ferry I've ever taken in which I've had a cabin. After chatting about politics and differences between the United States and Faroe Island peoples, the Faroese, we both retired to our cabins. It turns out the Faroe Islands guy upgraded to a private cabin while I on the other hand went for the ultra-economy option of a four-person berth cabin. Up until the first post it was just me and my Afghani roommate but when I got back I was met with two strangers dead asleep. If this had been three months ago this would have been weird, walking into a dark room with people you have never met then falling asleep. But after the amount of hostels I've stayed in and the number of times this very thing has happened I've gotten used to it. The earplugs went in and the little light went out and it was good night for me.

Upon waking this morning I met the guy sleeping in the bunk above me. A nice, bearded man from Iceland he too reassured me we would make it to the frozen north. The issue, he said, was not so much the snow, "Iceland can handle the snow," but the intense wind. Apparently the wind is so strong that it is throwing rocks and breaking car windows and stripping the paint off of cars. I told him my plan about taking a bus to Reykjavik and he said I will be fine. Once again, the locals are extremely confident in us arriving, it seems to be just a matter of when.

12.6.2015

1:28 PM

We've stopped. The ferry was going unbelievably slow since we began at 10:30 this morning and it turns out that was planned. Now we are halfway between Frederikshavn and the jetting out point on the northeast of Denmark, essentially safe from the open water. The game plan, according to the announcement of the intercom, is we are going to stay here until midnight then make our way to Hirtshals, with the planned arrival time being five in the morning.

I've explored the ship a bit and have been let down on the amenities. Like my luck with trains, it's always the short duration transports that have everything you need but the long ones have nothing. This ferry has super expensive food and drinks, the cinema (which on other ferries has always been free) costs so much to watch out of date movies, but there is one shining beacon in all this; the tax-free store. These are common in Europe especially in countries with ridiculously high sales tax. I ended up buying a six pack of Faroe Islands lager for $7, a steal when considering one can sold at the diner is $3 by itself. Once my treasure was bought I went to the very top and found a nice covered area with no one around. I sat down, opened a beer and began reading in peace.

Another problem, the gale is getting worse.

A gale force wind is something like greater than 45 mph wind blowing across water. Up here on the top of the ship the wind is howling and that is not an exaggeration, I have not heard wind like this since fishing in Alaska. The ship is stopped which means the entire thing is rocking back and forth with a vengeance. Luckily I don't get sea sick and I'm on board with Scandinavians which don't seemed phased by the weather in the slightest. There is comfort in reading a book and drinking a beer in an enclosed, Plexiglas enclosure while outside the elements are raging. There is also solace in the calm everyone has around me, anywhere else in the world this would be a frantic situation but these people are descended from Vikings and they start worrying until the beer is gone.

12.7.2015

10:19 AM

We're heading to Torshavn, Faroe Islands! Early this morning around three I woke to the boat rolling and rocking and knew we were on our way to Hirtshals but with bad seas. I went back to sleep with a letdown feeling in my gut and was fully anticipating waking up to the announcement of cancellation. When I got out of bed at 9:30 the ship was slightly rolling and I knew we were at cruising speed. Taking a shower and getting dressed in the complete darkness with no windows to look out sheltered me from the realities of the outside world. Opening the cabin door I hurried to a window and was greeted with a relatively calm sea and sunlight, the first true sunlight I had seen since London! A smile ran across my face and I went to the message board: *Arrival at Torshavn (Faroe Islands) Tuesday at 6:00 PM, Departure 7:00 PM.*

So. If all goes to plan, which there is absolutely no telling, we should be to Iceland no later than Thursday. The only problem with planning out here is this is the North Atlantic in December. Storms could pop up any time and totally derail our plans for further advancement. But, the ferry captain was confident enough to take on cargo trucks and begin the voyage which costs money and time so there has to be a plan with some kind of certainty in making it to our destinations. And, if all else fails I will get to at least *see* the Faroe Islands, not enough time to get off and explore, which will make me happy anyway.

12.7.2015

12:01 PM

Free food! A large Icelandic man came up to me just after I had eaten my meal of peanut butter sandwich with "Cool American" Doritos and explained to me how this ferry operates. "If we are more than six hours delayed from our destination time the food in the diner becomes free!" The man defined jovial and made a semi-waddle bee line toward the buffet. Thinking how bad his timing was I contemplated if I should take up the free food or be content with my meager meal…the answer didn't take long to present itself.

Whenever food is free it usually isn't the best quality and I set my standards low as I followed the hulking Icelandic man toward the buffet line. I was completely wrong. What lay before us was a beautiful display of fish, potatoes, steamed carrots, and the makings for spaghetti Bolognese. Keeping in mind I had just eaten a meal, I took some of each and savored each bite. It was so good to have a proper meal, something I have only had a few times on this trip in order to save on cost. My Afghani roommate came and sat next to me and we discussed how his day had gone yesterday and after we finished eating we decided to explore the ship.

On the very top deck, where I had been the day previous, he showed me a steel door that led to the front of the ferry. This is my fifth ferry on this trip and I have yet to be able to go to the front of the ship, I'm not entirely sure we were allowed up there but the view was spectacular.

The sea is so calm today and the wind almost non-existent, completely opposite to the past few days in Denmark. Once we ascended the stairs we were met with southern Norway stretching for as far as we could see on the right side, starboard, of the ferry. Taking out my phone I pulled up Google Maps and got an idea of where we were in the world. Norway was jetting out to our right, Denmark was to our lower left and the Faroe Islands were directly ahead; times like these always make me smile.

We were sailing in the heart of Scandinavia, the same route taken by many a sea goer for however many centuries. Whenever someone had asked me why I was taking a ferry to Iceland instead of flying I knew the answer was what I was seeing right then. How many more times in my life would I look at a map and see where I am right now or go to the top deck of a Danish ferry, look out and see Norway stretching as far as I see now?

12.8.2015

10:17AM

The worst storm since 1991 is happening right now in Iceland. All the roads are shut down, there are massive power outages and the rescue workers have been told to ONLY go out if the situation is life or death. Currently we are halfway between the Shetland Islands and the Faroe Islands, officially in the North Atlantic and the seas are calm and the sun is shining. This is the nature of weather, constantly changing and always unpredictable.

Last night before dinner my Icelandic roommate, Viktor, came over and sat next to me. I had been struggling to write a story for the better part of an hour and I finally got it going. Because of this I was a bit short with him in talk but he was patient and I decided talking to an Icelander was more important than writing a story. I closed my tablet and he gave me the news he had heard.

"It looks like we are going to make it! Last night I was talking to some Faroese guys, drinking whiskey until five this morning, and they told me we had two options. The first, we would miss the storm and get to Iceland late Wednesday night. The second, the storm would stick around and we would have to hang out in the Faroe Islands for a week." He said the last part with a smile, the same kind of ironic smile the entire boat shared because they knew no one could control the weather and there was no point in making a fuss out of that understanding.

For the next hour we talked about the storm happening and how people in Iceland were taping their windows to prevent them from blowing out and he showed me videos of car wrecks and road conditions. The entirety of Iceland is shut down until further notice and will take a bit of time to get back to normal. I then asked him the logistics of getting from eastern Iceland, the point the ferry would drop us off, then onto Reykjavik and he took a deep breath with big eyes and stroked his blonde Icelandic beard.

"It's not an easy trek. To get out of Seydisfjördur you must first climb a winding mountain road, steep and sketchy. Once that is done you must go down it, and if it's icy then it is even more dangerous. Within a few hours you will get to a small town called Egilsstadir which has an airport which I suggest you use to make your flight. If you don't then the roads to Reykjavik are slow and tedious, we have shit for public transport. Since you have a deadline I would recommend the bus, the bus won't get stuck and those drivers are completely used to these kinds of drives. From Seydisfjördur to Reykjavik will take about 12 hours, give or take a couple." With a shrug he grabbed his beer and took a long drink.

For the hundredth time this trip I felt like kicking myself out of my naiveté. I drastically underestimated the size of Iceland and their road systems. Thinking maybe six hours to cross, I figured even arriving on Friday morning wouldn't be that big of a deal. My search for adventure sometimes puts me in situations with which I have no control and these are disturbing sometimes but always fun retrospectively so I keep doing them. Like Louis L'Amour said, "I believe adventure is nothing but a romantic name for trouble."

As the conversation dropped off for contemplation between myself and the Icelander we both checked our phones and saw it was almost dinner time. Our Afghani roommate came over and the three of us went to dish our plates with some traditional Danish food and a beer, all for free! Sitting down we got to talking about our backgrounds and what we do and how we came to be on a ferry heading to Iceland.

Before starting I understood that I was the only American on the boat. This has happened a few times during the trip where everyone else around me is local but I am "the American" and it feels extremely good to have that position. I told them about my Alaskan fishing and my trip around Europe and mountain climbing and school. Like most they seemed surprised at how many interests I have and I felt good to share some stories from the Europe trip I was soon to be completing.

The next to share was Viktor, the Icelander. At 34 years old with blonde beard, short on the sides and combed back top for hair, thick frame glasses, and wool socks his mother had knitted for him he was nothing short of the stereotypical Icelander. He explained his art to us and showed us some pictures, it was astonishingly good. A kind of abstract realism, or realist impressionism, he melded real life animals and landscapes with abstract ideas within them. They were quite beautiful and he was impressively talented. Studying in France mostly and painting in Iceland gave him his unique flare for color and realist subjects. He was heading to see his family for Christmas in a small town a few hours south of Reykjavik while he worked on art projects he had thought up on his travels around Europe.

The Afghani was a shy man. With English being his third language I think it was out of self-consciousness why he didn't speak as much as the Icelander and I, which is a lot. The Icelander asked him how he came to live in Sweden and what we got was an astonishing story. "I was born in a small village in Afghanistan and had an okay life there. I was teaching adults when I got captured by the Taliban. They had me for a month and they made my father pay $20,000 to get me out. Once I got out I escaped to Iran and met a girl. We became close and we had some nights together and she got pregnant. Her father and brother told her they would kill me so we decided to escape into Turkey.

"The borders of Iran are dangerous because there are no guards but trip wires which if your foot goes past them they start shooting. We got shot at many times but it was dark and they couldn't see where to shoot. We paid some people at the Turkish border to get us through and we made it to west side of Turkey. At night 40 of us got onto a small raft with a motor and drove across the water into Greece. Once my girlfriend and I got to Greece we bought tickets to Sweden and we have been there for two years."

The Icelander and I were stunned. "I can't believe we just heard that story in person," Viktor exclaimed taking his glasses off and rubbing his eyes. I was almost speechless, only able to "yeah, that is an amazing story" or something stupid like that. The Afghani went on, "Once I get back from seeing my friends in Reykjavik I want to write a book about my experiences so people know what is going on in my home country."

I nodded my head and told him how great of an idea that was and how I would read that book absolutely. We asked him how he liked Sweden and if he ever felt threatened being there or if he would ever consider going back to his home country. He explained, as long as the Middle East keeps using Islam as their main religion there is no hope for peace there. Starting off as a Muslim, he said they were taught to despise anyone who wasn't Muslim and to strike them down whenever he saw a Christian. That is why he converted to Christianity and adopted the name Adam as his Christian name, Muhammed was his birth name.

It was obvious the conversation was getting heavy for him and his eyes began to tear up and his voice began to crack. Viktor reacted wonderfully and told him "let's not talk of those things. They make us sad and we are very far from Afghanistan and all that bullshit. You know it is going to be cold in Iceland, yeah?" With that we all three began laughing and the situation became easy going and joking between three men on a boat heading into a storm in the North Atlantic.

Both the Icelander and Afghani began feeling the symptoms of sea sickness after a while and the Afghani decided it best to head back to the bunks to lie down. We all went back to the cabin and I got my last can of beer and my jacket and Viktor and I decided to head to the top deck to see what we could see on the open sea. He had heard we were getting close to some huge Norwegian oil rigs and wanted to see if we could get a glimpse of the shooting flames in the dark, crisp air. Not able to see flames we only saw green and yellow lights spotting the distance and knew what they were.

Being on a boat in the darkness is one of the most soothing things I have ever experienced. It happened for the first time in Alaska when we would drop anchor in an inlet somewhere and turn the engine off. The silence was absolute and the subtle rocking of the boat was as good as any mother's arms rocking a babe to sleep. When out to sea there is a similarity. Only being able to see a short ways out, the entire world seems so far away, so empty. There is nothing to worry about because the isolation is so absolute. There is nowhere to go and nothing to do but talk to other passengers and try to pass the time.

Viktor and I found a seat under a heat lamp and opened our beers. Before long an extremely large Faroese man, one of the men Viktor had been up drinking with the night before, sat down named Jakob. Probably in his late forties the man was hulking as so many Scandinavian men are. Jakob was drunk and working on a joint but he was clear enough to formulate sentences and make jokes about the ferry sinking and comparing it to the Titanic. There was that humor I was beginning to get used to, the never-take-it-seriously humor they use to mask or deal with the stresses of being on an unforgiving sea in December. The three of us began talking about all manner of things until we got onto Jakob's history and I was blown away.

The man defined the badass Scandinavian. Before he was on this ferry he was in the north of Norway training dogs and dogsledding but he had to sell all his dogs due to a knee injury and head home to the Faroe Islands to see his wife and daughters. He told us stories of when he was a sailor on cargo ships all across the North Atlantic including brief stints crossing near Greenland and docking in Gloucester, Massachusetts and how it was a disaster for the seas were so rough the cargo would be beat to shit by the time they arrived there. After a few more beers we got back on the topic of dogsledding and his passion for it came out as strong as anything.

"It's the greatest sport in the world. The bond between man and dog is so strong. They have a love for you and you for them. They would do anything for you. I remember one trip we were in Norway going through trees at night and I looked down at the GPS and saw we were going 36 km/h and then the next thing I knew I woke up surrounded by my dogs. I had fallen off the sled from exhaustion and they turned around and surrounded me. I woke up in a fur blanket and was in heaven. Usually the lines get tangled and this wouldn't work but for some reason that one time it did and it saved my life." Jakob told the story so simply but with vigor and the truth of it came through gleaming. There was no need for adjectives or powerful verbs, he just told the story as if no one was listening but we all were.

He went on to tell me about his biggest ambition in life, to circumnavigate the globe on dogsled. My mouth dropped. How amazing is that? This is the year 2015 and there are people out there with ambitions like that. It seemed to confirm all my crazy ambitions which were nowhere near his in scope and everyone kept telling me to reel mine in and focus on smaller goals. This man wanted to be the first to go around the world on a dogsled and with his demeanor and truth in his stories I could absolutely see him doing it. Amazing people like that exist in the world today and I hope they never go away. Real people who have ambitions that are spectacular and fly under the radar and truly want to conquer a part of the world before they die. It's an old way of thinking and one the world should hope it never loses.

The rest of the night was spent drinking more beers with some Faroese guys and listening to one of them play some American songs on his guitar in an empty bar. At one in the morning the bar closed and we all said good night and retired to our rooms. As I crawl into my bunk amidst the snoring of my roommates I lay awake thinking of the stories I had heard from a few miraculous people. It confirmed my satisfaction in this part of the world and made me happy I chose this form of travel. The possibility of missing my flight on Friday is increasing but as of now I'm okay with it. Safety is first but closely second is the voyage and this voyage has been one of the main highlights of my trip thus far.

12.10.2015

5:06 PM

    At 5:30 PM on December 8th we arrived in Torshavn, Faroe Islands. It was to be a quick offload and go so none of us could get off the ship and explore like so many of us thought. I was okay with it, the quickness meant the people in charge had more than aspirations of making it to Iceland and my confidence increased. Earlier in the day my Icelandic friend came to me and said "we are going to make it to Iceland by one o'clock tomorrow. This is lucky since they thought we would have to spend a week in the Faroe Islands waiting out a storm!" By this time I was nearly immune to these kinds of statements, they stopped bothering me and I had come to accept the fact there was at best a 50% chance I wouldn't make my flight home on Friday.

    Everyone went outside to watch the Faroe Islands get closer and make out the beauty shrouded in the darkness. Torshavn is the capital of the Faroes and its population is only around 15,000 but the way it is situated it seems much larger. Everywhere we looked, no matter the vantage point on the ferry, it seemed there were houses engulfing every inch of the land. Some of the Faroese guys I had been talking to for the past few days started getting proud of where they came from and told me a rushed history of the islands and how they had "boomed" the past decades. It was nice to see strong men get emotional about where they came from, in fact it is nice to see men of that caliber show any emotion at all and when they do the ground shifts and light shines through the cracks and everything seems a bit brighter because of it.

The Icelanders who remained and I said our goodbyes to the Faroese wishing them luck and happy holidays. A few of us stayed on the top deck drinking Faroese beer and chatting about the beauty the small town below possessed. The layout of the buildings was most definitely Danish influenced, reminding me so much of the Nyhavn district in Copenhagen with its multi colored facades accentuated by bright white windowsills. The numerous shipping containers and freight filled with frozen fish came out from underneath us soon followed by people and their vehicles. The wind was becoming arctic and it blew with a bitter gust and all of us decided to go back into our viewing area and await departure.

Those who were left, perhaps no more than twenty, sat in the viewing area and talked about the plans each had once they arrived in Iceland. Viktor, the Icelander who I had been talking for the past two days, broke the conversation with "where is Adam going?" I looked up just as our

Afghani roommate walked by the open door with suitcase behind him and two large, plain clothed men on either side as if to escort him. Giving myself a push, I jumped from my seat and ran to ask him where he was going. I was too late, only seeing the last glimpse of him as he turned the corner of the exit ramp. "I bet that was the last time we will see him again," said Viktor with sincerity and a matter-of-factness so prevalent in his culture.

The ferry departed Torshavn around eight o'clock and the rest of the night was spent with the two of us running through scenarios in which the Afghani could have been taken off the boat. After a few beers and many a run through we came up with a basic solution. His status in Europe was most assuredly a refugee or immigrant one and he probably took the ferry to skirt around any kind of strict border control Iceland would have. Unfortunately for him, and maybe fortunately for us, Torshavn had a strict customs situation and he probably got questioned and once he couldn't produce the proper paperwork he got asked to leave.

The story he told of us of leaving Afghanistan sounded true and the way he broke down about his safety concerns seemed extraordinarily real but no one ever knows who people are when traveling and all of that could have been a lie. On the other hand, Iceland is known for being exceptionally sensitive with people of Middle Eastern descent and it might not have been a coincidence that the only non-Caucasian person on the boat was asked to leave. We will never know.

As I was heading for the cabin to end the day the night's weather forecast came over the intercom, "winds gusting up to 45 mph with 18 to 20 foot seas." I smiled with a bit of masochistic enjoyment from the rough weather and crawled into the bunk with glee. Throughout the night I awoke several times getting moved up and down with an occasional crash from the bow slapping the sea. It was a long night, not from sea sickness but the knowledge we were getting closer to Iceland and I had absolutely no concrete plans on how to reach Reykjavik. My nerves were frayed from the past week of not knowing and so many times that night I woke in a cold sweat not knowing the future. Hard to sleep with that cocktail of emotions.

Waking the next morning I felt terrible. My stomach would not settle from the anxiety. No matter how hard I tried I couldn't shake it. With the ship still going through rough seas the entire cabin would heave unexpectedly and jolt me to one side or the other. I was cranky and irritable with it all and rushed out to find a window to take in what I was sure to be a beautiful view.

I sat in my normal spot in the viewing room with no one around and heard we would arrive to Seydisfjördur around two o'clock that afternoon. A group of Icelanders came in and began their usual dialogue, the same the older men of all cultures do, and I tried to ignore them and read my book having no want for any interaction with my terrible mood.

Lunch time came and I decided to spend the ridiculous sum of $20 for one meal, it was salmon and tasted amazing but the ships prices were just out of control. Viktor sat next to me without food and told me he had been talking to an older Icelandic man who was planning on making the trip to Reykjavik as soon as we landed. I couldn't believe my ears. All morning I was trying to work out bus and plane fares with each being amazingly expensive and each leaving me stranded in super small towns overnight. My spirit perked and I finished my meal to meet the man.

    The man was standing in the viewing area looking to be around 60 years of age with an athletic build and earnest eyes. We shook hands and without hesitation he accepted me as a passenger. I offered to help with gas money but he refused telling me conversation was payment enough on the twelve hour ride across the country. I thanked him profusely and went back to my cabin to pack my bag and get ready for departure. Amazing how traveling works sometimes. For hours I had been stressing about money and time and if I would be able to make the flight on Friday when, within a few minutes, I secured a free ride as soon as we docked. The people you meet are amazing all over.

The ferry entered one of the eastern fjords of Iceland around one o'clock and the view was astonishing. All the young travelers went to the top deck to battle the icy cold winds to get a view of the miraculous nature all around us. The sun was beginning to get low in the sky and shone with a red intensity through the clouds and cast a pink hue complimenting the blue of the sky. We passed small farms right along the water so far removed from the nearest town and I couldn't help but smile at how remote they really were.

Around two, the ferry docked and I found the man who was giving me a ride and we descended the stairs towards his car. I said goodbye to Viktor and thanked him so much for talking to me throughout the voyage and connecting me with a free ride. We shook hands, exchanged information and I hopped inside the vehicle heading west.

A cross between a truck and a van with burly tires and a tough exterior, the vehicle had all the makings of something fit to thrive in Iceland. The Icelander introduced himself as Einar and at first I thought him a bit odd but I got a good vibe and we trekked onward. We made a quick stop at customs then took off on our expedition around 3:30 PM, expecting our arrival to be somewhere around four in the morning into Reykjavik.

The first hour or so was filled with the basic conversation of what we do and where we come from and what put us on the ferry in the first place. The roads were okay along the beginning but soon became icy which gave way to fairly deep snow. Both of us commented on how odd it was for the main road we were on to be so neglected. We shrugged it off and kept our conversation going until we saw a Subaru Outback parked in the middle of the road. It was completely dark at that point and we hadn't seen anyone else on the road so we were a bit weary when a man in a black trench coat and puff ball stocking cap came trudging through the snow at us. He told us he was stuck and didn't know what to do.

Unfortunately Einar had just bought the behemoth we were traveling in and had no towing equipment to pull the man out. We tried for some minutes to push the stuck car out of its resting place to no avail and finally Einar told the man, with his wife and seven month old baby, to get in with us to go to the nearest town.

    Along the way Einar called a few of his Icelandic friends and found the road we were traveling on had been closed since the storm began on Monday. Luckily there was a shoreline road we could take which would skirt us through some fjords but would get us to the west with ease. We dropped the three from the Subaru off at a police station and made our way to the proper road and began our voyage.

    We lost light a couple hours earlier so I couldn't quite get a good look at the scenery I knew was amazing around us. I kept bringing up the Northern Lights and, like most Icelanders, Einar told me we wouldn't see them for this reason or for that reason but I didn't give up hope. Early on he told me his history of photography and I instantly became intrigued. When he was in his early twenties he went to university to study the science of photography and worked for some time archiving historical photos and working in the film processing field. After that he started a few businesses, all involving photography in some capacity, and finally in 2008 started a photo-tourism business. Because of this his knowledge of Icelandic nature photography was brilliant and we talked about ISO and aperture and the best combinations to photograph different scenes.

    After a while he handed me his iPad and showed me photos he himself had taken over the past couple years. They were astonishing. As I have so many times in my life, my brain stopped and I took a second to understand how I came to where I was. What are the odds I would be traveling with an expert photographer through Iceland?

I noticed a green haze forming over some mountains on my side of the road and mentioned them to Einar but he discounted them for something else. Within minutes the dull green became ferocious and stretched across the sky in a brilliant scene of Icelandic beauty. Being a photographer he immediately pulled over and told me the specs to set my camera in order to get the best shot. Neither of us had a tripod so I tried using the hood of the truck to get a clear picture. The wind was too strong and it rocked the vehicle just enough to cause the ten shots or so to be blurry. We gave up and headed on down the road. Having been extremely lucky back in September, I had seen the Northern Lights on the plane approaching Reykjavik but failed to see them the next three days I was on the land. That night the sky was so clear and the green so vibrant I couldn't keep my eyes off of them.

Both of us settled into our seat, giving up the prospect of getting a shot without a tripod until we turned a corner and we saw "The Shot." Einar pulled over and I grabbed my camera, running across the road to a fence post which had a level top. Without being able to see where the lens was really facing I eyeballed it and took one picture. Feeling the pressure of so much road ahead of us, I decided one was enough and ran back to the truck and we took off. The picture turned out brilliantly for not having a tripod, for me never having shot Aurora, and for the unforgiving wind. To me it is amazing.

The next several hours were spent with Einar and I discussing every facet of our lives trying to avoid the miles which lay ahead. The roads were amazingly clear and we sped on with no difficulties. At one point, after the conversation had died out, the Icelander slammed on the brakes and startled me. "You've got to see this!"

Pulling off the road into a completely empty gravel parking lot I wasn't sure what there was to see. Maneuvering the truck to the edge of the lot so the high beams shone bright ahead Einar smiled and said "this is Glacier Lagoon, I take all my clients here!" What lie ahead was a floating glacier field as far as I could see. Each glacier was vastly different from the other. Some were big and blocky while others had been worn to points and spires. They were everywhere and even in the darkness I could notice the deep blue within each glacier. I tried to snap some pictures but the light just wasn't bright enough. Some photographs are best left in our heads.

We left the lagoon and within an hour it began to snow, then the snow started coming down even harder and back home we would call it a blizzard. Einar wasn't the least bit phased as he slowed his speed down and kept in the tracks of an 18-wheeler we had been following for some time. It was at this point, somewhere around one in the morning, where I started to doze off and on. I felt bad sleeping but he gave me the okay and I was out.

I woke as we were passing Selfoss, the eighth largest town in Iceland and the place my friend from the ferry would be heading the next day. This marked the half hour left mark until Reykjavik and I still had no idea what to do about the upcoming day. Normally I book my hostels at least a day in advance but with all the uncertainty marking the last week I didn't want to risk wasting money.

Consequently, I had nowhere to stay and it was four in the morning and I was thinking of ways to get out of paying for two nights pay. Anywhere else I would have found a café and spent the day walking around but the temperature was in the high twenties and it seemed ignorant to not have a place to call home.

Searching through all the resources my travels had taught me I couldn't find any hostel open past midnight and Einar wasn't offering me a bed at his house, nor should he since he had already saved me $200 on travel already.

As we were entering the capital Einar asked with a bit of an irritated tone, "what should we do here?" On the verge of frantic I remembered back to my first night of this trip and getting to a hostel at 2:30 in the morning and hearing a couple girls getting in at three. Deciding to roll the dice I told him to go to that hostel.

We arrived and the entire place was alight and my heart rose. I rang the bell three times and no one came, as high as my heart had risen it fell even harder. Now what? I climbed into the truck and began to think, it was then a girl ran to the door and told me they were open and I was ecstatic. I grabbed my bag and thanked Einar for everything he had done the past night and we shook hands and he told me to keep in touch.

At the reception the girl told me there were openings in every room but I decided to book a private one. The entire trip I have chosen the cheapest option no matter how much

I didn't want to or how tired I was but it was five in the morning and it was my last true day in Europe so I decided to treat myself. I have not slept that solid for some time.

Chapter 20

Home

Once checked-in, I walked through the quiet hostel to a small private room. As the door closed behind me the journey I had just undertaken began to set-in but it was five in the morning and all I wanted was to sleep. Dropping my things to the ground, I fell onto the bed, clothes and all, and passed out.

Around ten I woke with blue skies and snow greeting me out the window. I smiled and thought back to the gigantic circle the past three months had been. The next day I would be boarding a plane taking me away from the continent which had been my home for three months, away from the tremendous journey I had undertaken, and back to the home I was not yet ready to reenter. After experiencing that kind of freedom for so long, the prospect of going back to a normal life seemed foreign and absurd. I checked my plane ticket anyway and sent my mom an email, regardless of the heady thoughts racing through my brain home was home and it beckoned.

With a strange apathy I left the hostel sometime in the early afternoon to walk around Reykjavik. It wasn't that I didn't want to be in the city, I sincerely did, but the finality of the trip was immense and weighed strangely on my shoulders in a way which manifested itself in a kind of stagnation of emotion. The snow crunched underneath my boots, the same boots which had treaded across Austrian Alps, over sandy beaches, and through countless bars, as I made my way toward the Hallgrímskirkja, the sloped church which had been my first tourist destination of the trip.

Stopping for only a moment a flood of visuals washed over me. Using Icelandic money to pay to get to the top, renting the car, traveling through the countryside, it was all there in a flash. As I continued onward little things triggered these visual memory rollercoasters. They made me nostalgic and left wanting to go back to that person those months ago, filled with worry and anxiety of what lie ahead. The person who was standing in those same boots was different, he had seen things and learned things and was completely confident in whatever obstacle stand in the way. I had left that anxiety behind and replaced it with a feeling of conquest and, strangely, a feeling of been-there-done-that about Reykjavik. Perhaps it was because I knew how easy it would be to find another adventure, how easy it was to jump on another plane and fly anywhere else in the world.

Throughout those thoughts, I had kept wandering over the slippery sidewalks and found myself in the shopping district amongst the throngs of tourists gazing into the shops admiring trinkets and postcards. I bought a few last minute souvenirs, found a quiet spot for coffee, sipped slowly, then wound my way back to the privacy of my hostel room. With scarf tucked tightly around my neck I watched the sunset droop slowly over the hills extinguishing the light from my last full day in Europe. The next several hours were spent compiling notes, making lists of stories to write, and drinking cheap, low-alcohol beer which tasted like it had come from a lame sheep.

Morning came as it had the previous 94 days, full of light and promise. I checked my flight information, everything was on time. The sky was blue and the weather crisp. I ventured once more into the innards of Reykjavik soaking up the last hours of Europe. Back at the hostel I sat in the common room with my ragged daypack, which had turned into my only pack, while I waited on the airport shuttle to pick me up. As I sit there in the quiet serenity of finality a group of young, fresh-faced Australians burst into the room having just arrived. The juxtaposition of their air of adventure couldn't have been more different than my feelings of something which had come to an end. They sat behind me cracking beers and pouring over the map of Iceland which lay before them. Their emotions were magnetic and infectious.

    I turned around and started a conversation with them, as is common in the common rooms of all the hostels I had been, and talked about their plans and how long they were planning on staying in Iceland and other trivialities of travel which to those involved couldn't be farther from trivial.

All of us laughed and got giddy with stories and proclamations and promises and before long my shuttle driver walked into the common room to see a bunch of young fools drunk off their own journeys. I said goodbye to the people in the Icelandic hostel's common room and wished them all the best and safe travels. We had known each other for less than an hour but it felt like a bond which had lasted years.

    The drive to the airport wasn't long as we picked up six other passengers and skirted the countryside and the ocean. My eyes were glued on everything all at once, I wanted to be sure I soaked every bit of Iceland in as I could, trying to maximize my last hours of the trip like a greedy addict savoring the last drops on the bottle.

    I walked past the baggage spot which had been the impetus of my bag loss months ago, made quick work of the airport's security, much easier sober than severely hungover as I had been before, and found my terminal with plenty of time to spare. The plane was on time and I found my window seat. Before I knew it the plane was soaring and I watched the ground grow smaller beneath us as we flew northwest, it was to be a seven-and-a-half hour, non-stop flight over the north pole and into Seattle.

    Since we left at 4:30 PM Iceland time we would be time traveling at the exact speed the time zones were changing which meant the beautiful pink haze of just-before-dawn cast its light over Greenland, eastward through western Canada, soaking the mountains of northern Washington, until darkness fell and the Seattle lights flickered near.

The plane touched down onto the tarmac and shuttled smoothly to the gate, my heart raced, I was home. With passport clenched in hand, I nervously walked to customs. The experience entering the UK had scarred me and for many agonizing minutes I shuffled my way toward the customs agents worrying they wouldn't take me, sweating over all of the possibilities of not getting to go home. With a simple sign I scanned my passport through an automatic machine and was granted access to America. The flood of relief shot through me like a kind of adrenaline injection as I bounded down escalators and past people I deemed too slow.

The next flight was from Seattle to Portland. Through the night's darkness I stared out the window watching the blinking light on the plane's engine flash then light up the downpour of rain around it only to dim then repeat the action. With my music blaring and not wanting to sleep, I stared at the spectacle with burning eyes.

The next leg of the trip was on a much smaller plane, one with exposed engine blades of which I had never actually flown, which flew us from Portland to Pasco, Washington. The man next to me was a seasoned business traveller and we spent our time drinking complimentary beers talking over one another in great excitement about all manner of things. Turbulence hit a few times sloshing our beers but not getting in the way of our stories.

Our small plane landed in the ever-smaller airport and I wished my compatriot the best as I hurried off the plane onto the wet tarmac of the Pacific Northwest. With legs racing and eyes burning from lack of sleep and excitement at being home I climbed the steps, hurried through the mostly empty airport with sleepy janitors going about their business and airport staff leaning on elbows. I turned around corners, passed through gates, and with a start saw the meaning of home. With teary eyes and big smiles my mother, grandmother, and sister were standing there waiting for me. Tears welled in my dry eyes as I reached for my mom and gave her a great hug. We all embraced and smiled wide. It was official, I was home.

We drove to my grandmother's house in a cacophony of noise, mostly my sleep deprived brain trying to make sense of the world around me. I asked how the family was doing and they asked how I was feeling and told me how skinny I looked and kidded me about having some kind of bed lice from the hostel beds of Europe. It was a car ride full of nervous laughter, an expression of the relief we all felt. Relief on their part was obvious, I was home safe, but my relief came from making it all those miles back to the sanctity and normalcy of my vision of home which had not one ounce of feeling different.

 We arrived to my grandmother's house and I smelled the perfumes and pleasant odors of meals prepared perfectly and saw the antique cookware and pictures hanging on the walls, the same ones which had been hanging since I was born, and truly felt the adventure had ended. My brain wouldn't shut off as the clock neared midnight. I was jet lagged, my eyes were burning, and I had been up for over 24 hours. All of us hugged tightly and departed for our rooms.

They had given me the enormous king sized bed and I stripped down to my underwear, unclipped my long, greasy hair and laid down stretching to eternity. I had not been in a bed even half that size for over three months.

Grabbing my phone, I sent a few messages to friends letting them know I had made it home safely then switched to a timer app which I had started the minute I had left my grandmother's house to go to the train station three months earlier. Every minute of that clock had a memory attached to it. As I laid in that oversized bed I looked back on each of those days with zero regret. Before I left I told myself to take advantage of every day, every opportunity, always say 'yes' to adventure and 'no' to trepidation. I held myself accountable to those guidelines and as I laid in that bed looking into the darkness I was overjoyed with the outcome, immensely impressed at the adventure I had undertaken, and not at all saddened by being home.

The clock kept counting up as my thoughts veered from one extreme to the next until finally I stopped it. With a quick screen capture I solidified my trip in a few simple numbers. The exact length of my European adventure, the one time in my life thus far where I allowed myself to be completely free, and gave myself room to roam, was:

94 Days. 3 Hours. 24 Minutes. 23 Seconds

Chapter 21

Epilogue

Sometimes, like a cliche, I have to pinch myself to make sure I'm not dreaming.

Every morning I wake up, get ready like I always have, and leave for work. Before exiting the door I walk into the darkness of my bedroom and bend over to kiss my wife and baby boy. The two of them look so peaceful, so completely in love, and, above all else comfortable. I stand for a few more seconds taking in those moments, moments I already understand are fleeting, moments I know I will never be able to get back. The morning greets me with whatever season it feels fit and I walk out of the home we share, the same home my wife's mother grew up in, and leave for work, a job I had dreamed of having since I was in junior high.

The drive is long but worth it to provide for my family and to help make a better life for the baby who seemed so far away in the fall of 2015 when I embarked on the Europe trip with Reed. The girl who I was with at the beginning of this story, the one who split-up with me to go our separate ways, the one who unintentionally spurred me along the path of self-discovery that was that trip, she is now my wife and rightfully so. For the better part of nine years, in 2018, we have been together through highs and lows, small apartments with roommates, distance while I was playing fisherman in Alaska, through the rigors of college, the stresses of getting married, and the voyage of pregnancy that culminated in our child's birth. Through everything we have remained strong and our love for one another has grown, and continues to grow, with each and every day.

This love culminated when our son was born, a process I was fortunate enough to have a literal front seat for and catch him as my amazing wife pushed him into a world which can sometimes be harsh but mostly beautiful and full of wonder. The three of us huddled together on the bed of the nineteenth-century farmhouse which was his birth place and embraced every second together, feeling the power of our own family and the importance and responsibility that entails.

We came back to our home and have continued raising him since, watching with amazement at every milestone and smiling gleefully at every new sound he makes and the curious twinkle lighting up his blue eyes. These scenes would have never been possible without the schism which caused my then-fiancee and I to go our separate ways and her be her own woman living alone doing whatever she wanted to do with the freedom and irresponsibility of a mid-twenties woman in the twenty-first century. As for me,

I chose a different route, a route which shone through with all the idiosyncrasies of my personality and arrogance which rears its head in times of my deepest insecurities.

The trip to Europe began in the hop fields of western Oregon with a thought and a yearning to see the world, to test myself, and to find some kind of edge I knew had to exist. In Alaska I thought I found the edge while fishing in twenty-five foot seas, waves crashing all around me and a kind of raw, primeval joy and feeling of being truly present. Yet, like the sea, the edge I thought I had found was only the high water mark, each adventure seemed to push that mark a bit higher only to recede back into me and show me there were higher plains to reach. Through college the experiments, the papers, the cadaver dissections, the books read and the conversations argued, these were all pushing the high water mark a bit more above the horizon seemingly into the clouds then to come back to me with a foam and a ripple. It wasn't until Reed and I bought those plane tickets to Iceland when the seas began to churn and a storm began to brew, one which might just yet push that tide farther than it ever had before.

With each new country came different challenges, people changed and languages changed but the result was always the same. A new place meant temporary trepidation which quickly gave way to an acceptance and an understanding which taught me something new, something I will hold with me for my entire life. It is that newness, that novelty, I believe is at the essence of travel, an exposure to something so different from a person's norm that they can't help but expand and grow, become able to swell with the beauty that comes from understanding someone else's human experience and share in the wonders of the world.

This experience doesn't have to take place thousands of miles away from home, it can happen anywhere a person feels like they are leaving their comfort zone and feel that familiar frantic notion of anxiety, a twinge of fear, but lurking beneath these animalistic emotions is a very human curiosity and desire to see more, experience more, do more. That is the seed of adventure, the precursor to something bigger than any of us and something all of us, to varying degrees, yearn for. I was fortunate enough to find myself in a time in life where I had the freedom to roam, freedom from responsibility I do not have now which makes me cherish that time, only a few years ago, when the only person that mattered to me was myself.

The summer of 2015 found me twenty-six years old, single, without a permanent home, working a job I thoroughly enjoyed with a group of friends who I did everything with. There was no one needing me, no one watching me, only me doing whatever I wanted, when I wanted, and, for the first time in my life, I took full advantage of that freedom. I couch surfed from friend to friend, drank almost every night, worked long hours making as much money as I could, and saying "yes" to every opportunity.

Whenever I had a day off I would travel to the mountains, to the ocean, anywhere there were green, open spaces, anywhere there was room to roam and be wild to feel freedom and to embrace my home state of Oregon as much as possible. I spent as much time outdoors as possible during that summer and when I was at work I would find any opportunity possible to wander off into the hop fields and feel the humidity increase the deeper into the twenty foot tall hops I went. It was a magical summer, a time which would culminate with my best friend and I tromping off to Europe.

Over the course of the many pages of the book above I dwell on specific details; how places smell, the way I observed people, the way different aspects of a place caught my eye. This is not to drone on but to help share the experiences, the way I see the world, with someone I don't know, at least not yet. In my every day life, even after three years, a certain smell will fill my nostrils and the olfactory bulbs of my brain will catch fire and my memory will take me back to a coffee shop or a florist or a bakery in the small town of České Budějovice. It is truly amazing how travel affects a person, the confidence it instills, the beauty it exposes, the expansion of mind the whole experience brings forth.

For all of this I look back at those 94 days in the autumn of 2015 and smile. I have not one once of yearning for that time, I am fully content with the life I have now. In fact, I would trade every experience I had, every small town, all the intimate conversations had with locals, all the amazing food and sights in all of Europe for the chance to watch my son be born into the world again, to see the pure love and happiness in my wife's eyes as she held him for the first time, to feel the hot tears well up in my eyes as I caught him in my hands after that final push.

What I have learned from the last few years, the time spanning from self-imposed homelessness, to roaming through Europe with only a backpack, to marriage, the birth of my child, and the life of a supporting father is each chapter of life is beautiful in its own way. Within that chapter are the bumps and tumbles, desires for something more, and the occasional feeling of blessedness of the situation, which, unfortunately, happens quite rarely.

Once we leave that chapter of life, and only in true hindsight, can we observe ourselves at different periods like a telescope seeing daily life on a distant planet and truly appreciate the experience we had being alive in those moments. When I find myself daydreaming of the times had in Europe whether it be while I'm working in the microbiology laboratory or along my commute to work or when my son is crying and my wife and I feel defeated, I try to frame it for what it was and remind myself that life is good.

The only rule I set for myself before leaving America and embarking on the grand tour of Europe was to *Be Present*. When I was twenty-one I got that tattooed on the inside of my right arm as a constant reminder to try to stay grounded in the moment, don't think about the things I hadn't done in the past or dwell on what might happen in the future, just try to do what feels right in the present. At the end of the trip when I was laying in bed at my grandmother's house, after everyone had fallen asleep and jet lag was beginning to rear its head, I looked at that tattoo and smiled wide. I stopped the timer on my phone, the one which I had started 94 days before in the exact position anxiously waiting to arise and begin the madness that was the Europe trip. Tears welled in my eyes at those two simple words and

I realized I had lived my life, at least for those three months, at the purest root of those two words.

I felt strong in the same way I had when looking up at a mountain of water rising above me in a boat in Alaska, in the same way I felt driving tractors in the wide open wheat fields of my home town and bailing alfalfa in the shadows of the Wallowa Mountains in eastern Oregon or dissecting a cadaver in the basement of my university. I felt strong because I *was* strong, I had pushed the high water mark that much further and was now watching as it's tide came in and I could only dream of the heights it would reach at different times in my life.

All of us need to feel that strength at some point in life and the only way to be strong is to feel strong, to get outside of our comfort zones and to feel ourselves swell with the essence of what it means to be human. Every one of us has that thing that makes us get out of bed in the morning, work that job, endure tiredness by staying up later than we should, hustling for something bigger, something greater. Whatever that thing is we should stand at nothing to reach it, to grab it, make it tangible and real and wondrous and utterly unique to us.

For me traveling to Europe and finding room to roam was one more stepping stone to get to something bigger in life, what is yours?

ACKNOWLEDGEMENTS

Thank you so much to the people who let me sleep on their couches on short notices:

    Michael, Zoey, James, Dallas, Brett, Connor, Lacy

The countless friends who bought me beers when I was saving up money to go on the trip.

The short acquaintances who shared their stories and offered locations and hostels and tips of where to go.

Thank you to my family for putting up with my ideas which seem so far fetched at the time but usually work out.

To my wife who worked through the madness before we wed and continues to be a loving, supporting confidant when I need her the most.

TYLER GRINDSTAFF

Tyler is a husband, father, biologist, woodworker, photographer, and bread maker living in Oregon.

Room To Roam is the first of many diverse novels in production. Tyler wants to write a novel in each of the major genres of literature, ranging from Historical Non-fiction to Science Fiction to Western and even Romance.

This is the work of Travel.

To follow Tyler and the rest of the Grindstaff Publishing team's endeavors go to grindstaffpublishing.com.

ROOM TO ROAM: THE PHOTOGRAPHS

A collection of over 300 photographs chronicling the 94-day journey through Europe detailed in the *Room To Roam* novel. Arranged in chronological order from the ice fields of Iceland to the towering mountains of Austria and through the canals of Venice, *Room To Roam: The Photographs* showcases a backpackers guide to the back alleys and rarely seen views not seen in any tour guide's best picks.

Available at grindstaffpublishing.com

CPSIA information can be obtained
at www.ICGtesting.com
Printed in the USA
BVHW030752140621
609522BV00005B/68